MW00810855

THE **MAGIC** OF **MANIFESTING** **LOVE**

15 Advanced Manifestation Techniques
to Stop Chasing, Start Attracting, and
Become Magnetic to Your Dream Relationship

RYUU SHINOHARA

The Manifestor Masterlist
(It'll be near impossible without this...)

This Masterlist includes:

✓ Top 3 daily habits to maximize your manifesting abilities.

✓ Simple layout to track your progress.

✓ Instructions to help you get started today!

The last thing I want is for you to read this book and forget everything you read…

Let's make manifestation a daily habit!

>> Scan the QR Code above with your smartphone
to receive your free Manifestor Masterlist <<

Table of Contents

Introduction

I t is an innate human need to love and be loved. You have likely heard countless people utter it before. Maybe the words have even sprung from your own mouth … "I just want to find *the one*."

If you are reading this, then chances are someone you thought to be 'the one' turned out to not be so after all, or you have sadly suffered loss in your life from that loved 'one,' and believe there is no other. Alternatively, you are here because you feel a yearning for that connection that can only be shared with what is often referred to in popular modern literature as your *soul mate*. We have all felt it.

Nowadays, though, it may seem very difficult to find the one. To meet that one magical person who will sweep you off your feet like a knight in shining armor, or that unbelievable woman who will soften your heart, smooth your rough edges, and care about you like no one else before. Although a knight in shining armor or a woman who seems too good to be true may be stretching it a bit for anyone's reality, the truth is that it is not impossible.

This book will form an integral part of healing your perspective around love. To do this, you need to know that this will involve

1

healing yourself as well - the most important part. When this personal healing occurs; when you have acknowledged and worked on healing the beliefs you have of yourself; you will have achieved the most important goal. Only then have you overcome the biggest obstacle to truly becoming magnetic and drawing your perfect match towards you.

WHAT IS TRUE LOVE?

It can be the most magical feeling you've ever experienced, or it can turn into the worst nightmare and make you question the reasons for living any further. It can give you the strength and willpower to steer you through the most difficult times imaginable, or it can pull you down, into your darkest, deepest, most depressing lows.

What am I talking about?

Relationships. Love.

Nothing compares to the feeling of being in a caring and loving relationship with someone who sees you as a uniquely wonderful and beautiful person. When you first fall in love, not even the sky is the limit. It may feel like a never-ending daydream where everything feels perfect. Every moment is an eternity, and when you spend time together, it may feel as if you are conversing with a reflection of yourself. One mind in two bodies. A perfect connection.

You rarely notice any flaws because you're in such a high vibration that nothing negative ever crosses your mind. There is no substitute for that feeling. Nothing else compares.

"Love makes possible the miraculous, without labeling it miraculous."

– Dr. David R. Hawkins

The above analogy may be difficult to take in. After all, the fact that you are reading this book likely indicates that the explanation above is what you are searching for in a relationship. The truth is, you deserve to find the relationship of your dreams. You deserve to be happy. You don't have to live life alone or even feel lonely. This book is going to show you how – no matter how 'bad' you think things may be looking right now.

You CAN attract your dream relationship once you know how the universe really works. The journey you are about to take will lead you through all those seemingly hidden rules of the universe. What you will need however, are not only words, but also tools to achieve this seemingly elusive goal that will enable you to attract your soul mate, twin flame, or that perfect connection you have been wanting to manifest.

Like many, you may be going through life believing your past relationships have damaged you beyond repair. What this book will help you to realize is that EVERY SINGLE RELATIONSHIP - both good and bad - that you have ever had, is a blessing in disguise.

Yes – you read that correctly. Even those bad past experiences can actually help you attract your perfect match.

Take a moment and think about it. Can something bad produce anything good? Can a dreadful and heart-wrenching experience give birth to something pure and divine?

Yes, it can.

Together, we are going to dive deep into the practical applications of manifestation, stemming from the principles of the Law of Attraction. You will gain valuable insight on how to become magnetic to the relationship you've always dreamt about.

That's the bottom line. That's the ultimate goal. And I will lay down every single little detail I have learned in my life to help you avoid the pain and struggles that many people go through.

In this book, I'll share everything there is about the hidden secrets behind human attraction. I will share every little thing that enables people (whether consciously or unconsciously) – and that includes YOU - to finally attract that perfect person into their life.

It doesn't matter what gender or race you are. It doesn't matter what your sexual preference is. Your age and the number of past relationships you have been in are irrelevant. If you want to attract that one special person into your life, this is the journey for you.

The same rules of manifestation apply to all of us. What I can tell you with absolute certainty is that when you understand how it all works, others will notice. It will seem to them as if you have the magic touch.

Throughout this book, a secret will be made available to you that not many receive. You see, it all boils down to understanding the true reality behind successful relationships and attraction. In other words, while it may seem like magic to some, to others, it's just life. Because they understand the mechanisms. They know how it works. They are making the mental and emotional effort to change the way they think and feel to, ultimately, take inspired action steps and set it all in motion. After reading this book, you will be much better equipped to do the same.

T H E   A B U N D A N C E   O F   L O V E

For you to grasp how important this information is, you need to first hear the following somewhat harsh truth. You have to understand that getting involved and being committed to the wrong person for too long can stop you from living at the frequency of your desires.

Such a misdirected commitment limits your ability to attract amazing things into your life - things that exist beyond your relationship. That's exactly what makes this exciting journey so vital for you. It will set your life on a growth trajectory path by helping you avoid making the same mistakes that so many of us made while searching for a loving partner.

Then again, is there just *one* person for you? With over 7,5 billion people on this beautiful planet (divided approximately in half by gender), if you remove a billion of those who are already committed, you end up with well over one billion remaining people, conservatively speaking, waiting in anticipation to finally meet *the one*.

Knowing that, do you believe it's possible to have a "perfect relationship" with .01 percent (or 100,000) of those people? Wouldn't it be fair to say then that you actually have a hundred thousand potential soulmates instead of just one?

That's how you need to start thinking. I want you to realize that there is the potential for more than just one amazing relationship. That a failed relationship does not mean there are no more out there for you.

The word to describe this is *abundance*. An abundance of love and connection *is* possible and available to you, whether you believe it or not. This is where this book comes in. Helping you align and solidify a belief of true and limitless abundance is exactly the perspective you need to not only know and understand, but nurture. It will open you up to a whole new world filled with love. It's all around us. Once you begin believing in your self-fulfilling abundance, you will become aware of the attraction happening all around you.

MAGNETISM AND AVOIDING MISALIGNED MANIFESTATIONS

In reality, the feeling of 'being in love' for many is actually rather an unhealthy attachment to an individual or relationship. Avoiding this pitfall of a pattern of dependency involves setting standards and values from the start, *before* you even attempt to draw someone into your life.

With that said, being very clear as to what your dream relationship looks like is essential for avoiding ambiguity and misaligned manifestations. You have to know who you truly are and what you want. In other words, **set your standards and stick to them**. Do not compromise. This is not about you learning how to see every partner through rose-colored glasses and ignoring everything you don't like about them, or making excuses for them. Instead, this is about being specific as to what you want for yourself deep down so that the universe can do that familiar magic and finally connect the two of you. Your soul mate is out there. He or she is waiting for you to get into that perfect alignment with who you truly are so that the universe can initiate the attraction process.

A key point is this: It may sound rather ironic, but the more you don't *need* a partner, the more attractive you will become to one and the happier you will be in the resulting relationship. The more freedom you give yourself to think, feel, and act in alignment with who you are, the more freedom you give others to do the same. This is what it means to become *magnetic*.

It is my mission to make you embrace your true self; to embody this wonderful, amazing person that you are so that ANYONE would be lucky to have you. I want you to stop fearing being hurt, rejected or disappointed in love, and rather feel good about yourself while simultaneously radiating happiness everywhere you go. Most importantly, I want you to experience this feeling *now* - even without an ideal partner being in your life yet. Removing the victim mentality will be one of the primary goals of this book. When you finally *choose* to become a powerful, magnetic, attractive version of yourself, you'll never feel lonely again.

Does this mean I'm asking you to not really ever love someone? Absolutely not! Quite the contrary. **Once you learn to unconditionally love someone, you are effectively empowering yourself**. When you love without strings or conditions attached, you free yourself from bondage – from the normal relationship fears most people have. If this sounds too complicated or confusing, do not worry. This book will give you everything you need to learn how to do this.

YOUR PART IN MANIFESTING THAT MAGICAL CONNECTION

In working through this book, you will be required to think deeper than usual. You will need to carefully read and contemplate all 15 techniques. Pick a few that resonate with you best, and extract as much good feelings as you can out of them. This is how you feed your soul. This will come with the important realization that you're becoming fully equipped with everything you need to finally manifest that magical connection with another being.

We are going to get into some concepts that are going to challenge your entire central belief system and everything you think you know about attracting love. During this process, be prepared for me to ask you deep, probing questions - the answers of which are necessary to help you get a clear vision of what it truly takes to create your dream relationship. This is a vital part of letting go of the old, to make place for the new.

Before you realize it, you will be able to let go of the past negative relationships that have been keeping you stuck. This will in turn lead you down the path of a new perspective and understanding, resulting in the occurrence of a necessary internal paradigm shift. As a result, you will have enabled yourself to attract the right person. It's going to take a little faith on your part, but once you embrace the new reality, you'll never look at relationships in quite the same way.

If the above sounds familiar to you and intrigues you, I am confident that no matter whom you are; no matter what is going on in your life; no matter how dismal you think your relationship outlook may be - you're going to become the magnetic force you really are with the ability to manifest all of your relationship desires. You will be empowered, your mindset boosted, and ultimately, you will find what you innately seek … **THE ONE.**

"Love is the recognition of oneness in the world of duality. This is the birth of God into the world of form."

— Eckhart Tolle

CHAPTER 1

The Hidden Connections Between People

Intuitively, we all know that there is a hidden connection between people. Even if only subconsciously; we can feel it in the very fiber of our beings. Usually, the closer the person is to you, the stronger that connection may feel. This is why a mother or a father feels a special bond or a connection to their offspring, and likewise, children to their parents. But this connection is not only limited to families. It can go way beyond that.

You may meet someone for the very first time and feel a powerful, inexplicable bond towards them too – maybe even stronger than those held with family members. It may feel like your souls are somehow intricately linked; like they are at home with each other. How can that be? What could be the source of this? Is the myth of past lives possibly true?

In this chapter, we will explore the hidden connection between all of us. We will cover the connection between humans and the universe, and the most powerful law that brings it all together - the Law of Attraction. Using scientific evidence, we'll be able to explain this connection by examining the nature of how our reality works from a quantum physics perspective. Understanding the 'whys' and 'how's' of your reality will give you a broader view of the concepts you will learn about throughout this book. As a result, you'll be able to apply them with more conviction and confidence, ensuring that you attract the exact relationship you desire.

Before we dive into the connection between each other and the universe however, the most important connection that needs to be considered is the connection between YOU and yourself.

THE MOST IMPORTANT CONNECTION OF ALL

The importance of understanding the relationship you have with yourself cannot be emphasized enough.

All of us have a higher self, an inner being, or a soul, if you will. It is that part of you that could also be referred to as source energy, or the divine. This is the part of you that knows who you truly are and what you truly want. It's the unfiltered and unconditional expression of you.

From the secular perspective, this is called your *intuition*–that part of you that knows things beyond the realms of logical reasoning. This unique calling, that every one of us has, is connected to a wisdom that goes beyond what we can explain simply with mere words. It's infinite. When we recognize and follow this guidance offered by our intuition, we're put on a path which leads towards more synchronicities, success, fulfillment, and love.

This is why life coaches are taught to encourage their clients to "follow their own intuition," or to "go with their gut instinct." They know that this infinite wisdom springs forth from this connection with the source energy within us all, even though they may never really go too deep regarding what its source actually is.

The best way to refer to your unique expression of source energy is as your *inner being*. The term *higher self* is somewhat accurate, but this reference makes it seem like you are less than your higher self, when nothing could be further from the truth. You are indeed your higher self - you just haven't fully embraced it yet. The reason for this, in part, is that we have been raised by a society that limits our potential to consciously be the powerful and deliberate creators of our reality that we are.

For the journey that lies ahead in this book, it is important that you understand who you really are. Through this understanding, you will have the strong foundation needed in order to get the most out of life in every way possible when it comes to manifesting love.

Your inner being loves you more than you know, and it communicates this through your emotions. It is that non-physical, larger, older, and wiser part of you. This spiritual part of you has been with you since your birth. As mentioned earlier, the connection you have with your inner being is the most important connection you can have.

The truth is, if you were living in complete alignment with this part of yourself already, you wouldn't need this book. You would never feel lonely. The idea of lacking love would never cross your mind and express itself as a negative emotion. You would be able to manifest whatever you wanted to, easily and quickly, including a wonderful love relationship. Love would manifest with an ease and flow like you would have never experienced before.

Throughout this book, I am going to assist you to see life through the eyes of your inner being. When you start to see life from *that* perspective, life will become much more gratifying, with less fear of what may lie ahead in your life and relationships.

We will delve into more concepts around this later, but for now, let's talk about the nature of our universal reality. This will support and strengthen your belief around the link between existence and human connection.

THE CONNECTION BETWEEN HUMANS AND THE UNIVERSE

For over two hundred years, quantum physicists have known that the smallest particles known to man, subatomic particles, defy the Newtonian laws of physics in dramatic fashion.

One example of this was through an experiment called the Double Slit Experiment, performed by scientist Thomas Yang in 1801. You are welcome to research more about this experiment, but for the sake of understanding how quantum physics and manifestation are intricately linked, I'll explain some of the basic terms of quantum physics, and the outcome of this experiment in layman's terms.

Quantum physics is the study of the subatomic particles spread across the whole universe. It also explains how physical matter comes into being, as well as how we are able to influence and have direct control of this matter. As these subatomic particles, (of which everything - including you and I, exist), vibrate at a certain frequency, everything in the world is made up of the energy emitted by them. This energy movement creates the illusion of a physical reality, as if everything were a standstill and solid object, when in truth, it's just a collection of non-physical energy emitting a specific signature.

This is why Einstein said "*Everything* is energy." He didn't just say that hypothetically. He said it because that was what they found to be true. As Nikola Tesla also once stated, "*If you want to find the secrets of the universe, think in terms of energy, frequency, and vibration.*"

The Double Slit experiment involved seeing how subatomic particles reacted to being forced in a certain direction. The outcome? The particles behaved completely against what the scientists expected to occur. To see why this outcome transpired, they recreated the experiment, this time with a measuring device. The subatomic particles were thus being *observed* – and amazingly, they acted according to the scientist's expectations!

Numerous further developments have been made in quantum physics over the past two centuries. If all of the scientific jargon is removed, some of the outcomes of this initial experiment (confirmed further in studies since then), could be listed as follows:

- Subatomic particles seem to be able to make decisions based on the behaviors of other subatomic particles (they appear to have an instantaneous 'knowing' between them)
- Multiple realities/possibilities exist at the same time
- What the scientist (observer) *observed* offered the *reality* of the outcome, even though the previous (unobserved) outcome was different. In other words, what they observed became the reality created at that time of observation.

So how can this then be linked to manifestation of something desired in your life, such as a meaningful, loving relationship? It is important to remember, in this regard, that we are also made up at a cellular level of subatomic particles – which means that we also have a vibrational frequency that impacts other subatomic particles. Let me narrow it down for you:

- The power of observation offers the reality created. If you can picture a desired outcome, and think, act and speak accordingly (in other words, observe/acknowledge it in all ways) as if you actually have it, then your vibrational frequency will manifest that reality. It will become physical in your reality. It first requires your belief, attention, and focus, as the observer.
- Just as different outcomes occurred in the recreation of the exact same experiment, except that one was observed and the other not, multiple realities exist at the same time. The subatomic particles in the Double Slit experiment could make decisions towards the outcome, based around the movement and intention of other subatomic particles. Similarly, your

thoughts, decisions, beliefs, and expectations can and will determine which possibility or reality you experience.

- 'Coincidences' may actually be the manifestation of people, opportunities, and experiences caused by you, being drawn across your path to support you in making your desired outcome a reality. However, if you are not in alignment with this reality, these synchronicities will mean nothing to you and will pass you by as if nothing happened. In other words, the opportunity for the manifestation of your dream relationship could literally be right in front of you, but because you're not a vibrational match to it, the inspired action necessary to bring the manifestation to fruition would never happen. Remember - all subatomic particles are connected across the time-space continuum in the universe.

Ultimately, what this all means, is that when you set your intention (call it your desire or outcome if you prefer), the vibrational frequency which then emanates from you will influence all subatomic particles to be arranged in such a way that follows your intention. That's right – YOU set things into motion! Now that you know that, we can move onto breaking down the Law of Attraction.

THE LAW OF ATTRACTION AND LOVE

I am certain you are at least slightly familiar with the term 'Law of Attraction.' It is the law that states that things of a similar vibrational frequency are attracted to one another. Vibrational frequency has been mentioned above, and will be expanded on further shortly. For now, let's look at how the Law of Attraction influences our lives, and more importantly, our relationships.

The Law of Attraction is not a once off event. It is a universal law, meaning it is *constantly* in effect. There are moments throughout the day where we notice its effects, sometimes instantaneously. Have you ever thought of someone who you had not thought of in a while, and then suddenly, they called you? Or, have you ever felt really good, and then suddenly started experiencing a momentum of positive manifestations? The opposite is also true. Have you ever gotten out of bed in a bad mood, and then have everything go wrong for the rest of the day?

You have seen the effects of the Law of Attraction. It's an inescapable part of reality, which is why it's so important to truly master the concepts surrounding it if you desire to live your best life. There are many misconceptions around this law and contradicting ideas that lead people to believe it's not true. One of the most important things to understand, though, is that **you attract who you are, and not necessarily what you want**.

How so?

We live in a 'yes-based' universe. What this means is that whatever you focus on, you attract. This is an important idea to understand because if you have tried to get the Law of Attraction to work for you in the past, but it hasn't, this could be why.

What I mean by we live in a 'yes-based' universe is the following: whatever you think about, you bring about, whether you want it or not. The more you shout "No!" to anything in your current reality, the more the universe hears "Yes!" For example, if you shout "No to war!"- the universe hears "Yes to war!" If you shout, "No to bad relationships!" - the universe hears "Yes to bad relationships!"

Can you see why it's so important to understand how it works?

Whatever you shout no to, the universe hears yes. This is why most spiritual gurus will never be against something, but they will always be *for* something. They will not march *against war*, but they will march *for peace.*

Can you see the difference? It's all about what you think and focus on.

This is going to be very important for you to understand when you consider finding true love. The point is, when it comes to relationships, **you must focus more on what you want and less on what you don't want**.

From a practical perspective, what this means is you should avoid, to the best of your ability, talking about and identifying with past negative relationships or experiences. Why? Because once you've tuned into the frequency of that experience, you've begun the process of shifting into a reality that resonates with that experience. This is why it is best to avoid complaining about an ex-partner to a potential new one - it not only activates the old vibration, but you risk closing off the possibility for a new love relationship.

Have you ever noticed how you or your friends seem to attract the same kind of person over and over and over again, even if you don't want to? That's the Law of Attraction in action. This is why understanding vibrational resonance is so important. Once you master your state of being, when it comes to relationships, you'll embody magnetism so powerful that you will inevitably manifest EXACTLY the type of partner you want to attract.

It can be difficult to avoid resonating with a negative past you are so adamantly convinced you need to identify with. You may dread making the same mistakes, and thus be constantly reminding yourself of what you *don't* want to have reoccur in a relationship.

You have to stop those patterns of thought here. You have to get over the urge to constantly rehash those negative bygones. In this book, I will show you how.

VIBRATIONAL FREQUENCY

Vibrational frequency is the foundation of attraction. It is the energy we emit into the world and we attract into our physical experience based on the signature of this energy. Our vibration (energy) has a unique frequency (signature). This is what creates our own unique vibrational frequency that manifests our own unique reality.

Our vibration is determined by two things: our thoughts and emotions. When you think a certain thought, it causes you to have a certain emotion, and when this becomes a habit, the reverse can also occur. Certain memorized emotions will start leading to certain thoughts. These events create a vibrational frequency that is emanated out into the universe.

Something that confuses a lot of people is the idea that a high vibration results in the manifestation of what you truly want, but this is not always the case. A very happy and positive person can be single, just as a very sad person can be in a wonderful relationship. This is why it's so important for you to tune into the right frequency of precisely what you want in order to attract it. The same way a radio station releases electromagnetic waves (vibration) from one signal to another, you need to practice tuning into the station (frequency) that plays the music you want to listen to.

The point is, if you have resistant thoughts about something specific you want to manifest, you can't manifest it, whether you are generally happy or not. Our thoughts play a big role in this and they can be broken down into three sections: beliefs, patterns, and awareness.

Beliefs

In simple terms, a belief is just a thought you keep on thinking. But it's a little more than that. It's also a set of crystallized perspectives that have been confirmed repeatedly from past and current experiences. These experiences then produce an emotional response that leads to a deeply rooted truth about your reality. For example, if you had a negative experience, or multiple experiences, where a person has let you down, you may be convinced that all people will let you down.

The problem is this…

You create your reality based upon what you believe, because when you believe something to be true, you will *unconsciously live* at the frequency of that reality. You start embodying this state of being naturally, and thus your vibrational frequency slowly begins to manifest the reality where all people will let you down.

A belief can also be described as entrenched thinking. It is a set of thoughts that you have thought over so many times that it has now become like a worn pathway through a meadow. In other words, it has become a truth of your life. Although it can be difficult to rewrite this truth, it's not impossible.

Patterns

Patterns of thought are the result of solidified beliefs. They too are perspectives you have thought many times over before. The perfect example of this is driving. Most people drive without any effort at all because they've done it so many times before, it's become second nature. Any thought can become a pattern of thought, if it's repeated enough times. If you find yourself facing the same problems over and over again when it comes to relationships, you may have unconsciously developed a pattern of thought.

Both beliefs and patterns are not necessarily bad things, but they can be if they are strengthening a perspective that isn't in alignment with what you truly want. But just like you can create negative patterns, you can also create positive ones that reinforce the vibrational frequency you want to be emitting. The goal of this book is to redefine your perspectives around love and relationships in order to break free from the patterns that repel them.

The first step to breaking free from the chains of negative beliefs and patterns is through awareness.

Awareness

The advantage human beings have over all other mammals on Earth is we have the ability to be aware of ourselves. We have the ability to be aware of awareness, and aware of who and how we are being, what we are doing, and how it affects us and others around us. It's an amazing ability that should never be taken for granted.

We can practice awareness right here and right now.

Bring awareness to a negative belief you might have. It could be anything. It could be about men or women, dating in general, or relationships. It could be something like "all men hurt me," or, "no woman ever likes me." Whatever it is, shine a light on it. If you can't yet figure out what it is, no worries, let's go through a quick exercise.

The simple act of being aware of what you believe is the first step to making a vibrational change. Once you identify it, then ask yourself the question, "Which of my perspectives is forming this belief?"

Once you've identified the cause, it's time to look at the "why" you hold this belief.

In many ways, beliefs are formed because they serve you in some way. Sometimes beliefs are formed to protect you from getting hurt or from changing who you think you need to be in order to receive love from others. Once you realize a specific belief is something you no longer want to hold onto, you've taken the first step to making the shift.

Your perspective is usually formed from past life experiences, but let me tell you something now. The past is exactly that, the past. And once you start resonating with an experience that no longer serves the manifestation of your current desires, you block yourself off from the natural growth and expansion of the universe. This is what leads to negative emotions and a state of being that is stagnant and completely out of alignment with your inner being.

Resonate with a *future* self now, and make the intention of creating the experience you want consciously, instead of unconsciously letting experience create you.

We'll talk more about the specifics of putting actions into place to let go of these beliefs in a future chapter. For now, let's see what it truly means to manifest a loving relationship.

THE MANIFESTATION OF YOUR DREAM RELATIONSHIP

The manifestation of your dream relationship starts when you realize that **you are the creator of your reality**. If you think otherwise, you'll never allow yourself to play with the magic at your disposal. You'll allow circumstance to define your life and relationships for you. If your circumstance is far from ideal, and you believe that it will never change, then you'll continue manifesting circumstances that are far from ideal. This, in turn, will have an effect on your relationships.

There is no other way to look at it. When your emotional state of being is consistently radiating a certain vibration, you are consistently tuning into a certain frequency. Master your state of being, and you'll master your reality. Your thoughts, emotions, and beliefs play a huge role in this.

Whatever you believe about relationships is what you will create. It's really up to you! This is why it is so important to choose to have good, solid, positive beliefs about relationships.

Judgment, blame, jealousy, guilt and a feeling of unworthiness are all feelings which have negative beliefs as their basis. These will keep you from attracting the relationship you want. Judgment can be either internal or external. Guilt and unworthiness are examples of internal judgment. Blame and jealousy are examples of external judgment. At the end of the day, these all reflect what you think about yourself.

Emotions come in only after you've decided on your new perspective. Emotions are defined as 'energy in motion.' Because of this motion, emotions are never what you might call *stable*. They will always fluctuate up and down. This is especially important to realize because our emotions are what connect us to other human beings. This is why relationships involve such a strong emotional commitment. The goal here is to not hold your emotions in one state forever, but rather to accept and effectively manage them when they arise.

Whenever you are feeling really down, it's impossible to instantly snap out of it and suddenly start feeling joyful and happy. Instead, take small steps up the emotional scale. Choose to view these negative emotions as a sign that you are not in alignment with your inner being. What this means is that your *perspective is misaligned from your truth*. In other words, you're depending on external conditions to make you feel happy, instead of feeling like you have the ability to create or manifest better external conditions. Remember - manifestation starts from within!

You have a *choice* to think and feel how you wish. This is the choice of watering the seeds of your desires.

"To grow your garden (change your reality), you must guide the flow of water (emotions) using the garden hose (thoughts)."

– Ryuu Shinohara

THE FREQUENCY OF LOVE

It is mentioned above that our vibration (energy) has a unique frequency (signature). The frequency of love is very high. It is one of the most sublime feelings we can experience. Many people have tried to define what love is. Regardless of any given definition, we can all agree love is one of the best feelings a person can experience.

The problem with most of us is that we have a distorted view of what love is, based upon our own experiences, and influences from society and the media. Many movies portray love as something external or extrinsic, and that we must 'go out there and find it' in order to be happy and satisfied. Often in movies, a sense of being incomplete is portrayed, until that seemingly perfect match occurs towards the end.

The problem most of us get ourselves into is when we think love is something we *receive* from someone else, rather than *create* within ourselves. When you think of love as an external, conditional entity you must work on in order to have, then you

26

are going against the very tenets of the universal laws that attract it to you.

When you realize that love makes up the underlying non-physical aspects of who you are, with or without another person, then you have understood what love truly is. This understanding will help you to not only attract more of it from others, but *be* more of it as well. Love is the ingredient that makes up your true nature. You do not need to create or find it, because you *are it*.

Haven't you ever noticed how people who seem the most attractive and magnetic don't go around chasing love? What do they do instead? They focus on themselves because they are confident in their own self-worth. This confidence may appear to be arrogance to some people, but the truth is, either knowingly or not, they attract love because they love themselves.

When you love yourself; when you appreciate yourself; when you enjoy your own company; only then will you attract it. That's the law. That's how it works.

Be it and you will attract it.

Feel it, regardless of your circumstance, and you will witness its manifestation.

Most people wait until conditions are right in order to feel good. "I'll be happy when my dream partner arrives. Until then, I choose to be miserable!" is pretty much what they are telling themselves and the universe. But can you now see why this is a fallacy? Do you understand why most people get stuck in a vicious cycle from which they seemingly cannot escape?

When you can love yourself, love life, love others, and love all that is, *regardless* of conditions - then you haven't just mastered the art of love – you have mastered the art of life.

TECHNIQUE #1: RELATIONSHIP CREATION

Ask yourself the following questions and contemplate the answers:

What do I want from a relationship?

How do I want to feel in a relationship?

For this technique, we're going to be answering these two questions. It's a simple, yet extremely effective technique simply because it puts you in the right vibration every time you do it. Your focus is purely on the wants and positives that will come from your relationship with another person.

The point is to write down not just 1-2 sentences, but rather a full page or two of the kind of relationship you want to attract and how you want to feel in this relationship.

Something you want to consider is how you feel about the different aspects of this person's life. For example, would you be open to playing volleyball if they were someone that enjoyed playing volleyball? Maybe they enjoy their quiet time and staying indoors. Would this be something you could enjoy with them too? **Define your unconditional perception of them.**

You want this person to like you for who you are, not for who you think you are. This is key because if you're not referring to your true self in these writings, you may vibrationally match with someone you don't truly enjoy spending time with. Instead, **write about how they make you feel.**

Be aware that being too attached to the extremely detailed specifics can close you off from infinite possibilities. This is why it's essential to focus on how you resonate with the person on a vibrational and energetic level. Use the details to make you feel a certain way instead of using them to outline a plan or aesthetic picture.

If you feel any doubt or tension while writing out the specifics of what you want to experience, start with general items. Begin with appreciating and believing in your ability to manifest, your connection with the universe, and the contrast that you've witnessed in your life that gave birth to your desire. When you've been thinking about what you've been missing for so long, it can be tough to shift into a whole new line of positive thought.

Start with general thoughts, work your way into more detail, and allow yourself to fully feel what it will be like to experience this relationship. Do not try to rationalize your thoughts, or you'll give room for doubt to creep in. Instead, allow the intuitive flow of your truth express itself through your writing.

Take time now to write these things out.

TECHNIQUE #2: THE RELATIONSHIP FEELING

The Law of Attraction is based on the vibrational frequency you're emitting. Your vibrational frequency is determined by your emotions but guided by your thoughts. For this technique, we're going to be focusing on elevating your emotions so you can enter the positive state of attraction that will allow you to attract the kind of relationship you're after.

The key to manifesting the relationships you want is not about focusing on the physical representation of the relationship, but rather the *idea of the relationship*. "What's the difference?" you might ask. The difference is that one focuses on the manifestation and one focuses on the feeling. Instead of looking at the relationship you want from a place of lack, look at it from a place of abundance. **Allow your imagination to be the reason why you feel good.** You do not need the physical manifestation of it in order to feel what it's like to have it. Here are the three main reasons why getting joy from *the idea* is powerful:

- Prevents you from getting attached to and vibrationally influenced by physical reality.

- It's the easiest way to get into alignment at any moment in time, no matter where you are.

- You will focus less on the 'how' and 'when' aspects of manifestation. This opens you up to infinitely more synchronicities.

Be receptive, open, and allow yourself to receive the manifestation of a new or enriching relationship by becoming a vibrational match to it *now*.

"Every time you are tempted to react in the same old way, ask if you want to be a prisoner of the past or a pioneer of the future."

– Deepak Chopra

CHAPTER 2

Creating Clarity from Chaos

Out of the chaos and contrast in your life, clarity, direction, and resolution are born. When you can see the value of the 'bad things' that happen in your life, including bad relationships, only then will you begin to experience the emotional freedom that comes along with this realization.

Even relationships which had apparent negative outcomes have their own unique type of value. There is value in EVERY relationship you have ever had before, due to at least two reasons. Firstly, that relationship helped you gain more clarity around what you do want. Secondly, you created a more powerful desire than ever before to manifest a better relationship. You may be skeptical regarding those two explanations, but subconsciously, you know them to be true. This is why you are here reading this, after all.

Let me explain. Ironically, most of us head into every relationship thinking that this is the one – the one and only person we will ever have, who will save us from a life of everlasting unhappiness and loneliness. We become so attached to the idea of being in a relationship that the thought of not being in one becomes something viewed as a negative in life. When we pass through the 'rose-colored glasses' time period, either partner may start feeling disillusioned with how the relationship is going. Before long, probably after numerous disagreements, emotions vented and silent treatments; it's over. We are left feeling hurt, angry and sad, among a whole host of other negative emotions. It is understandable that very few of us can end a relationship and feel a sense of appreciation for it.

There is nothing quite as emotionally turbulent as getting involved in a relationship. We subconsciously allow our thoughts and beliefs to be influenced by our past relational experiences, and this affects how we show up in the present moment. We unwittingly allow negative thoughts from past experiences to define our future. This is what causes people to feel stuck in a never changing reality loop. It is why they constantly seem to attract the same kinds of circumstances. Another common scenario is self-sabotaging the relationships they do attract. All of this deeply rooted mental and emotional baggage needs to be cleared out if we're ever going to open up the windows to a new reality.

Because these negative relationship experiences are usually associated with a strong emotional reaction, these negative memories stick with us for a long time, until we decide to acknowledge them and let them go. Negative experiences usually involve heartbreak, and unsuccessful attempts at finding love. This includes toxic relationships, external judgment from others, internal judgment from ourselves, and false external confirmation that what we want is not possible. We become so attached to these ideas that they shape our sense of self or identity. The ego also plays a huge role in how we view relationships because it's the ego that keeps us attached to ideas that do not define our true selves. When you put all of this emotion and experience together, it creates a vortex of internal chaos.

WHY WE RINSE AND REPEAT RELATIONSHIPS

Why is it that many people get into unhealthy relationships that are reminiscent of or exactly like other unhealthy relationships they are familiar with? For example, if you have parents who have had a bad relationship, why would you attract a similar relationship, thus increasing the likelihood of having the same kinds of problems? Wouldn't it make more sense to form a relationship with someone who had the exact opposite traits of the type of relationship you *don't* want to experience?

If you have always been in relationships which tend to follow the same trend in either the type of person you have dated, the way you have related to the other person, or the way in which the relationship has run its course, then you need to hear this.

One of the reasons we seek out what we know, is that we form a comfort zone of sticking to what we are familiar with. Even though a 'comfort zone' can indeed cause much discomfort, it seemingly has a benefit. It allows us a reprieve from having to heal.

Because healing means acknowledgement first.

And acknowledgement hurts.

It is not a natural human instinct to cause ourselves pain, either physically or emotionally, so by default, our natural instinct would be to avoid it. Healing needs to occur before anything else. Some people may use dating as a form of avoiding the process of healing. You have to do the work on yourself, internally, before you can begin the work of finding someone else.

Why is healing so important, though? It is only through healing that we open ourselves up to vulnerability again. I will say that again. **The vulnerability that is required in any meaningful human connection will first require you to heal.** If you do not heal, you will end up self-sabotaging, as the emotion of vulnerability will otherwise scare you. For a meaningful and healthy new relationship, you need a foundation of confidence, self-love, and healing.

So how does this 'rinse and repeat' cycle of relationships relate to your vibrational frequency? This phenomenon is so common that psychologists have a name for it. They call it, *repetition compulsion.*

As the name implies, people who have repetition compulsion compulsively repeat the same experiences in life, whether they are consciously aware of it or not. Psychologists are not exactly sure why it happens, but from a metaphysical perspective, if you do not change your vibrational attitude relative to how you feel about relationships, then you will attract the same ones over and over again. **You can't attract a different reality with the same frequency that attracted the current or past ones.**

According to psychiatrist and researcher Bessel van der Kolk (2016), "Many traumatized people expose themselves, seemingly compulsively, to situations reminiscent of the original trauma. These behavioral reenactments are rarely consciously understood to be related to earlier life experiences."

If your self-esteem is low and you don't feel worthy, for example, you may purposely enter into a bad relationship because you don't feel worthy of a good one. This is not something any person would *want* to believe, it's something they've been *conditioned* to believe. You may even get into relationships just because of the fear of not being in one. In other words, you have low expectations you are prepared to settle for, for yourself.

If you seek out an external assistant to your healing, such as a therapist or coach, there is something you need to be aware of. Make sure that you are not simply seeing them for a venting session, to enable you to learn how to cope within your brokenness. You need to actually acknowledge and resolve the issue and heal from it. Sometimes, something as simple as writing a letter to someone who hurt you can be cathartic in this regard.

Reliving past traumas over and over again, in the hopes that talking about it will make it better, will only aggravate the problem if it's not coming from a new state of being. And now that you know how the Law of Attraction works, it makes sense. If you're going to talk about how bad past relationships were and wallow around in the mire of those low vibrational frequencies, then of course you're going to attract more and more negative thoughts and feelings. **Shift out of the frequency of the problem and start living in the frequency of the solution.**

Your inner being is the purest expression of love, but because your mind has built so many filters (beliefs) around whom you are and who you can be, you will usually unintentionally block yourself from radiating the frequency that would attract someone you have a deep and true connection with.

Let's break down these beliefs:

THE THREE LIMITING BELIEFS AROUND LOVE

Beliefs are powerful. Henry Ford once said, *"Whether you think you can or can't, you're right."* It's such a profound statement because in a nutshell, he tells you the power you have to create your reality – or not. It's up to you!

Here are three limiting beliefs that stop people from manifesting true love:

Fear of Having What You Want

This may seem like a strange fear to have. Who would be afraid to have what they want? But in reality, this could mean actually being afraid of losing what you want *after* attracting it. **It's the idea of preferring to avoid the pain of losing, more than embracing the possibility of having.** When you finally do get into a relationship, this belief can cause you to constantly be worried and therefore never fully present with your partner. You could be there physically with them, but not actually there, because emotionally and mentally, you're somewhere else.

The signal you emanate out into the universe when you think and feel this way is a vibration of lack. When people say they fear love, what they really fear is not having it. This thought process does not put the focus on the manifestation of the desire but rather on the absence of it. This is like believing you've already lost it before you've even had it. True manifestation only comes from stepping into the unknown. It comes from stepping into the frequency of the desire. If you're scared of being happy, then you're telling the universe you prefer to be unhappy.

Humans have a survival instinct that naturally tells them to avoid what is unknown and stick to what is known and familiar. This is related to what we've talked about earlier in this chapter. The unknown is usually framed as a dangerous place to be in, which is why most people avoid it. Manifesting a new reality requires you to step into the unknown. This is why it's called a *new* reality. Your current reality is old news. It's the manifestation of the vibrational signature you had in the past. In order to attract a *new* reality, you need to step into a *new* frequency, *new* territory, *new* thought, *new* feeling, *new* action, and *new* belief.

Be fearless in your desire to manifest the love of your life and want it more than the fear of not having it.

Shame and Guilt from Past Experiences

Usually, we feel guilt and shame from past events that we have never really addressed before, and this will have an effect on new relationships.

The difference between these two feelings is this: When we receive a negative evaluation from others with regards to either something we have done or not done, or around the way we look, to name just two examples, then that external evaluation leads us to experience shame. This could be linked to abuse, or cultural and religious norms. The depth of this shame will be dependent on many factors such as your sense of self-worth at the time, your confidence level, and who the comments or evaluations are coming from.

Guilt, on the other hand, is a negative reaction or expression towards *ourselves*. It is the feeling of having done, or not done, something that you believe you shouldn't, or should, have done. Having an ingrained sense of shame however, can certainly exacerbate a sense of guilt. If we feel that we have hurt someone in a past relationship, the sense of guilt may be holding us back from entering a new relationship, in case we hurt someone again.

These feelings of guilt and shame from our past have conditioned us to believe that this is who we are, though in many cases this shame is unacknowledged by the individual experiencing it. They may avoid relationships, suppress their emotions, and possibly either feel worthless or anxious, or even display traits of narcissism as a defense mechanism.

Knowing what you do now about guilt and shame, and especially if this has touched a nerve with you, you need to understand the following important point:

You've defined yourself through these experiences, thus creating an illusion of your identity. We can easily develop the belief that "Nobody wants to be in a real relationship with me" or "I mess up every relationship I'm in," simply due to the fact that we've experienced guilt and shame in relationships before.

Your past is nothing more than a part of your imagination now. It can never be repeated, unless you give it permission to by matching the frequency of such an event. Giving your past life story a meaning that disempowers you will only limit your potential for manifesting future desires.

We'll talk more about this later in the chapter. For now, know that shame and guilt are two of the lowest vibrational feelings on the emotional scale. Working to get rid of these emotions is essential if you're ever going to break free and manifest your dream relationship.

Not Believing in Your Ability to Manifest Love

If you believe that you do not have the power to manifest true love, this belief will stop you right in your tracks. Believing in your power to manifest abundance, of any kind, should be the first step to manifesting love. If you believe the love of your life doesn't exist, or you're not capable of attracting them, then you need to reframe this way of thinking.

Remove all thoughts of scarcity. Realize the power and control you have to purposely think better feeling thoughts in order to create your reality. The universe is abundant, and we have access to this abundance through our consciousness and imagination. Match the frequency of being in a relationship, not just by seeing it from a distance, but by embodying the person in the experience. **You can feel the feeling of having your desired reality right here and right now, even though physically, it is not yet present.**

When most people think about the idea of being loved, happy, and peaceful, they think it's something they have to search for outside of themselves. In reality, our natural state is a state of infinite potential, joy, excitement, love, happiness, and limitlessness. The only reason we do not notice it is because many of us have unconsciously layered it with conditions and limitations.

Imagine looking up at a cloudy sky with small patches of bright blue. The clouds are the limitations fogging your view, and the bright blue sky is you. Your only goal is to remove the clouds, one at a time, so you can shine through the limitless nature of your being - a nature that is extremely attractive to other people. But in order to remove these clouds, we need to rewrite the stories that created them in the first place.

HOW TO REWRITE STORIES FROM THE PAST

When it comes to changing your self-image relative to relationships, a powerful approach is changing how you look at your past. As time goes on, your vision of the past naturally becomes blurrier. And eventually, it gets to the point where we are making things up about what we experienced, when in actuality, we never did. Always remember, the past is now just a thought. When you change this thought, you change your past, and when you change your past, it almost instantaneously feels like you've become a new person. In this subchapter, we're going to be expanding a little bit on this concept and providing you with new perspectives around it.

Neutralize Your Negative Beliefs

The way to do this is to remove any attachment or label around the things that are holding you back. For example, if you have a freckle on your face that you think is ugly, reframe this belief by viewing the freckle as a small part of your overall uniqueness. See it as neither good nor bad. It's just there, and giving it more importance than it needs, will move you out of balance, and simply clutter your mind with negative beliefs about yourself and what others think.

Embarrassing or heartbreaking situations in the past may stop you from taking future risks. Redefine these moments. Humans have a unique way of creating the illusion that because the past happened, it must be true, even though it's now just a thought. The past is a thought, just like the future is a thought. And many times, we don't even remember the past correctly. Therefore, wouldn't you being the best version of yourself *now* be just as true as the worst version of yourself you seem to recall or assume as true? **The only real moment ever is now.** You can only decide who you were, and who you are going to be RIGHT NOW.

Regretting the past or worrying about the future are both two negative behaviors that are ego driven and only serve to create more mental and emotional chaos. Neutralize the disempowering meanings you've placed upon your life, and watch them slowly, but surely, dissipate.

An Opportunity for Growth and Recognition

The natural flow of the universe is to be forever expanding. In order for it to expand infinitely, there needs to be both chaos and order. Without one or the other, the universe would limit its potential for expansion. Think of it like demolishing a house in order to rebuild it again as a new and improved home. Every time you break it down and build it up again, you learn something new about the process and the pieces involved. Thus, every time you rebuild it, the result is better than the last.

The same thing can happen when this analogy is applied to your relationships. You can improve and build upon every new one you enter. View life this way and you'll find it easier to create more positive beliefs about everything in life.

Another way you can capitalize on negative situations is to use them as a way of gaining clarity around what you do want. If a negative situation arises and you're aware of this negativity, then you've confirmed that it is something you don't want, thus instantly creating more clarity around what you do want. Keep this in mind whenever you're facing any sort of contrast or challenge.

You Already Have Everything You Need

Recognize that what you want is already available to you emotionally and vibrationally.

How so?

What you really want is the feeling of what it would be like to manifest your dream relationship. You want to feel love. You want to feel that excited, happy, good, and euphoric feeling that comes AFTER falling in love.

The thing is - we attract based on the frequency we put out, and not the other way around. Therefore, we must connect with the experience and feel it *before* it is reflected in our physical reality.

In other words, you must feel the feeling of love and euphoria *before* you attract your dream partner. Every manifestation has a delayed effect in the 3D realm, but we have the opportunity to experience this manifestation in the form of a good feeling in the present moment - now! And actually, that's your only option if you wish to attract improved relationships, because it's how the universe works. You create what you want by living the experience FIRST.

Creating a feeling is a manifestation in and of itself. It's the only confirmation you need that what you want is on its way. This is what I mean when I say "you already have everything you need." You already have the ability to feel however you want to feel regardless of whether or not what you want to manifest is here yet. **You do not have to wait.**

When you think a thought, you access a field of consciousness. This field contains an infinite number of parallel realities you can tap into right here and now. Consciousness cannot tell the difference between physical and non-physical reality, just as your body and emotions can't tell the difference between a thought and real life. Do not allow physical reality to determine that you lack something, because physical reality only ever represents ONE configuration of reality. In other words, everything you have in your life right now is the result of the thoughts and feelings *from your past*. It's old news.

Your future is the result of the thoughts and feelings you purposely think and feel now, no matter what your current reality is. Decide to put your focus on the optimistic, positive ones, and watch reality begin molding in your favor.

TECHNIQUE #3: BELIEF HACKING

For this technique, you're going to embody the future version of you by rewriting your past. In other words, pretend like you've already experienced what it's like to be in love, be in a relationship, or be attractive and magnetic to people. Do not worry about the details.

An infinite number of realities already exist. Therefore, what you rewrite about your past using this technique reinforces your new identity. It is the truth about who you are becoming. Time is simply an illusion and it is not linear. It is malleable. The past, future, and present all exist in the eternal now. Therefore, you can see yourself as the product of an infinite number of pasts.

The mind cannot tell the difference between a thought and experience. Stop thinking about the past through the eyes and mindset of your old identity and start thinking about the past of your new identity. Use your imagination as your reference experience. A first, this may sound confusing to you. Let me clarify this through an example:

From the perspective of someone that is at a coffee shop and someone they are physically attracted to, is signaling them to approach.

Old identity: "I'm not confident enough to approach this man/woman. I've never done this before."

New identity: "I'm going to approach this man/woman because I'm confident in my ability to do so. I've done this before and nothing life-threatening ever happened."

Another example can be how you react to someone rejecting you.

Old identity: "This is typical for me. I'm not attractive or charismatic enough to attract this type of person. They are way out of my league."

New identity: "Oh well, seems like they're not interested. I have proof that other people were interested in me in the past. Let me spend my time focusing on those that resonate with my true self."

Simply by believing that you've *already experienced* all of the unknown territory that you will be stepping into, will give you the confidence to be yourself and handle the situation in a present state of mind. This will prevent you from overthinking, reacting, and being anxious about all the things that can go wrong. The idea behind this technique is to override your survival instinct of avoiding the seemingly unknown or forgotten, and help you to overcome your fear. As you start replacing the imagined experience with real-life reference experience, you'll find yourself becoming more accustomed to embodying this new sense of self.

TECHNIQUE #4: DESIRE DISCOVERY PROCESS

For this technique, we're going to place the focus on how you can use your reference experience to get more specific with what you want to attract. There are three types of people you can attract:

1. The one you don't want.
2. The one you want some of.
3. The one you want all of.

Our goal with this technique is to attract the third person. How do you know exactly what you DO want without knowing what you DON'T want? This is where your previous experience in relationships, no matter how subtle, will come into play. Remember that right at the start of the journey encompassed in this book, it was stressed that your focus should always be on what you DO want, rather than what you don't. This is only possible though, through acknowledging (but not obsessing about) past experiences that have not felt aligned to what and who you truly desire.

NOTE: As we've mentioned before, a perfect relationship indicated as 3) will come with imperfections. It's how you deal with these imperfections that make the relationship perfect.

Look back at the best times you spent with another person. What did you appreciate the most about them? Was it the intimacy? The humor? The intelligence? The fun? Write these things down. Shift your focus to all of the positive aspects you experienced with all of your past relationships.

This is what will help you build your vibrational signature. Avoid labeling past relationships as bad relationships. Again, remember that you can extract positives out of every single relationship you've ever had to help you build the desired relationship of your dreams. Once you know exactly what you want, you'll find it even easier to vibrationally align with it using the perspectives and techniques in this book.

Enjoy the moments you have in your relationships. Enjoy your expansive nature. Enjoy the new preferences you'll gain as you experience more and more.

"Never pretend to a love which you do not actually feel, for love is not ours to command."

— **Alan Watts**

CHAPTER 3

Hidden Thought Patterns
that Repel Love

When you know what thought patterns *repel* love, then you'll know what thought patterns *attract* love. Most of us have subconscious thought patterns that, not only make it nearly impossible to attract the kind of relationship you truly desire, but may also lower the quality of any future relationship you get into.

Children can often sense and feel the effects of the dysfunctional relationship habits their parents once had, and often times, repeat them. When they grow up, they tell themselves, "I don't want to be like my mom or dad." This is where things go wrong, because as discussed previously, when you try to *avoid* something (in this case, becoming like your mom or dad), you unconsciously manifest more of this reality into your life. Why? Because *your focus is still lingering in that frequency*. The goal here is not to avoid the wrong kind of relationship, but rather to attract the right kind.

In this chapter, we will deconstruct three main thought patterns that repel love. For each, we will discuss what it is, how it comes about, and how to fix it.

PEOPLE PLEASING

What It Is

People pleasing is the act of trying to satisfy others in search for a pay-off in the form of self-validation or attempting to 'earn' love. Some people manifest this in the form of putting other people's needs first ahead of their own, leading them to feel exhausted mentally, emotionally, physically, or even financially. The people pleaser usually ends up feeling under-appreciated. They have all the evidence in the world to prove their worth to others, and yet they never feel their actions being reciprocated. Despite this, they continue to do it because of the negative beliefs they have about themselves.

One way to identify a people pleaser in others, or even in you, is to notice how hard it can be to say 'no' when asked for anything. When you find it easier to constantly say 'yes,' regardless if it goes against your truth, you've unconsciously entrenched yourself in the pattern of people pleasing.

The ironic thing is that people pleasers, out of fear, rarely let the people they are pleasing know how they truly feel. And yet, the very thing the people pleaser seeks, which is acceptance, love, and validation, is commonly withheld because others recognize one important flaw: People pleasers do not stand up for their truth. In other words, they act out of alignment, and when you act out of alignment, it's very easy to notice. **When you disempower yourself, people can sense it.**

This mentality of constantly trying to meet the expectations of others in order to be liked and loved can drain you of your energy. It implies that you can only get love by treating people with a 'fake niceness' that goes against how you truly feel. This way of thinking also takes the power away from other people. When you constantly please someone, the recipient often times gets used to it. And this in turn, will not allow that person to discover the inner power they have to please themselves and form their own happiness. The pleaser ends up becoming the source of their happiness, which is draining to both people in the relationship.

The opposite is also true. If your source of feeling self-worth comes from pleasing others, you will feel unworthy when you don't. This can potentially lead you to being easily manipulated, and to act in ways that put you out of alignment.

Overindulgent parents can show the same traits and characteristics of people pleasing by doing everything they can for their children (sometimes called 'spoiling'), whilst not giving them the opportunity to fend for themselves in the real world. In the case of these kinds of parents, it may seem like they are simply being loving, but in reality, the child is being controlled and becoming dependent upon the parent. This also takes away the value of learning how to create one's own reality, which is the whole point of this book.

How It Comes About

This personality trait usually surfaces because one does not see the value in their truest expression. This negative belief is usually created in childhood and will carry over into adulthood if you are not aware enough to change it. It may surface from parent pleasing, where the child feels that the only way to gain their parents' acceptance and love is by doing everything they are asked to do. It may also have been a way to avoid conflict in a tumultuous household.

Society, parents, teachers, siblings, and friends can have a strong influence on how someone views themself. Thus, they develop the need to create this false persona that is constantly changing and acting out of alignment to fit within everyone's expectations. Subconsciously, people do this in order to get what they truly want: validation, approval, and external representations of love, rather than developing these feelings internally.

How to Fix It

If you suffer from this people pleasing thought pattern, know that you are not alone. It is a common phenomenon. It happens to many people because of the nature of how most of us are raised. You *can* overcome it.

The best way to 'fix' this is to first understand and realize that you are an eternal, powerful spiritual creator having a temporary human experience, and *you* are just as valuable from the eyes of source energy as *anyone* else. You are a unique and divine expression of that which man calls God - and so is everyone else. Therefore, you are identical in value. You have nothing to prove in this lifetime. You don't earn self-value – *you are born with it*. This can be difficult to accept or believe, with life circumstances and experiences possibly having cemented the false beliefs you may currently hold. You may have lived your whole life thinking the opposite. However, don't worry. We will discuss more on the subject of self-worth in a later chapter, but for now, I want you to understand this.

To put it in simple terms - please yourself! Only *you* can give yourself the validation you're looking for. How *you* feel should be your priority. There should be nothing stopping you from allowing yourself to feel love, regardless of what the outside world tells you. There's nothing wrong with giving to and helping others, but when it costs you your alignment, this raises red flags within yourself and to other people around you.

Value yourself and express your personality in an authentic way or people will never see the real value in you. If they don't appreciate your real value, then they were never giving you real love in the first place. Let go of needing validation and approval from others. Accept who you are and *own it*. Be the star of your own movie. Don't be the supporting actor in someone else's.

You are not being selfish when you put yourself first. In actual fact, when you are being your best, authentic self, you're actually *more* of service to others. Find and recognize a perspective that feels empowering and expansive. The manifestation of your dream relationship will come when you recognize that nothing 'out there' can ever fulfill the needs of what is within.

CODEPENDENCY

What It Is

Codependency is when someone is dependent or attached to a relationship (or the idea of a relationship) and uses it to confirm their sense of self or identity. In other words, feeling loved and whole is dependent on external conditions, whether you are already with someone or not. This creates resistance, because you're not radiating from your truth. Rather, you're defining your level of happiness based on how a relationship is currently going, how it went, or how it could be.

Why are we touching on this subject if the goal is to attract someone in the first place? I want you to understand the pitfalls of codependency and the effects it can have on your vibrational frequency, and thus on what relationships you attract. You will then become better equipped to attract complementary relationships, rather than codependent ones.

Codependency can occur in three ways: a partner that is dependent on you, you being dependent on your partner, or both. Have you ever subconsciously thought about the following statements when it came to another person? -

"I need this person to be this way so that I can feel good about myself."

"I'm going to do whatever they want me to, so they don't leave me."

"You complete me."

Once we look for reasons outside of ourselves to feel a certain way, we limit the potential of attracting all kinds of abundance into our lives. If you *need* the relationship, then you *lack* it vibrationally – or you wouldn't be actively seeking it out, or sticking through in a less than ideal relationship. If you don't need it, then you can attract it vibrationally. You attract everything and everyone into your life based upon the frequency you emanate out into the universe – and relationships are no exception. If you are or have been chasing validation and approval in unhealthy and less than ideal relationships, it's time to reconsider your approach.

Let me attempt to simplify this concept. A codependent person tends to chase what they want with a sense of neediness. They want people to respond to them in a certain way. In response, however, the recipient of their neediness will typically put out an energy of resistance, as they subconsciously feel that the codependent person is trying to take something from them. They can feel that a specific type of response is being expected from them, and no one likes to be controlled in this way.

You *cannot* force relationships, friendships, and connections in order to fill a void that is missing inside. When you chase love, you repel it. Nobody wants to be the rubber plug that fills your emotional hole, unless they are dependent on that too, or a people pleaser.

Codependency can manifest itself in the form of vicious cycles of breaking up and making up, even when abuse is involved. This is a very serious issue that can often be very difficult to overcome, but not impossible. I recommend you personally

THE MAGIC OF MANIFESTING LOVE

consult a licensed professional for a more personal approach if this is the case.

How It Comes About

Codependent, unhealthy relationships manifest because of the belief that love and happiness can only be found in someone else and not in us. The ego part of our consciousness is always *seeking* and *attaching* to ideas, things, and people in an attempt to strengthen an identity. It is the part of us that is preoccupied about the future… the part that says "What if this does not happen…what if I don't find love."

As mentioned above, codependent relationships are thus manifested when egoic thinking takes charge of your thoughts and emotions by attaching your sense of wholeness onto the illusion of physical reality.

Codependency comes from the deeply rooted idea that we are not good enough. This feeling of not being good enough can stem all the way back, again, to when we were children. Having our parents fulfill all of our needs, resolve all of our problems, and be the source of our happiness is usually where it starts (even if the parents have the best of intentions). The parent-child relationship is often one of reciprocal currency. In other words, if you behave in a certain way as a child, you will receive a certain reaction.

Past experiences can also be a determining factor in the manifestation of a codependent relationship. If being single was a terrible experience for you, the ego will want to avoid it at all costs, which can then eventually lead to manifesting a people pleasing mentality or attracting a bad relationship with someone. This can also be the case for those who have been in a relationship for many years. It can be extremely uncomfortable stepping into the unknown and experiencing something new, even if you intuitively know that it's the right thing to do.

Being codependent while in a relationship is harder to recognize than being a people pleaser, but recognition and awareness is the first step to overcoming it.

How to Fix It

Here are a few questions to ask yourself to help bring awareness towards the issue of codependency:

- Am I in any way dependent on a/this relationship – or *needing* a relationship?
- If I could go the next 5 years without being in a relationship with my dream partner, would I be okay with that?
- Do I allow others to compliment my limitless nature and do I compliment theirs?

The answer should be yes to all three, and if it's not, here's how you can make the shift.

In order to manifest the independent nature of your future dream partner, you have to first develop an independent nature within *yourself*. You have to develop enough self-esteem, self-acceptance, and self-love in order to have the strength to break out of having a codependent nature. Discover the areas in life where you find yourself being dependent on others and work to improve them. It can be tough to take up more responsibility, but sometimes you don't need to. Just letting go of the feeling of being dependent and attached to what others provide to you, is enough.

When you give yourself more responsibility for how you feel, you increase your *response-ability*. In other words, you become more aware of how you choose to think, feel, and act. This is a massive step to making the shift from being an unconscious creator to being a conscious one.

It's important to recognize the possibility that people can be addicted to being treated poorly or to the ups and downs that are so common in codependent relationships. If you want to manifest an exciting and expansive relationship, it's essential that you match this nature before you enter one.

Start focusing on yourself more. If you find yourself often blaming other people, take responsibility in how you choose to feel rather than blaming or depending on others to do it for you. You only need yourself to feel happy, loved, and secure.

A relationship that is built from two people who are both 100% whole is the ultimate alignment – the ultimate goal. In mathematical terms, $1 + 1 = 2$ (collective energy of two whole beings) versus $\frac{1}{2} + \frac{1}{2} = 1$ (collective energy of codependent people).

> *"If two lines are moving parallelly, they go on for infinity. But if they're focused on each other, they'll cross and they'll go far away from each other."*

– Gurudev Sri Sri Ravi Shankar

When we talk about the idea of manifesting a dream relationship, we're not looking to manifest just any kind of relationship. We're looking to manifest the BEST kind of relationship for YOU. Manifest a relationship that is *complementary* and *not* dependent. Be unapologetically yourself. Give up trying to control the outcome and other people's responses towards you. Know that the validation you may be seeking since childhood is already inside you.

UNWORTHINESS

What It Is

Unworthiness is one of the lowest vibrational attitudes you can embody. It's the feeling of not being good enough in one or many different ways. Examples can range from not being smart enough, not good-looking enough, not out-going enough, not talented enough, etc. It's that sense of self that feels limiting, constraining, and powerless - that feeling that no matter what you do or how hard you try, you'll never be enough to fill in the expectations of others or yourself.

It stems from the false premise that you are what you've done and how others see you. The problem with this sentiment is that it's born out of an attachment or identification to past experiences and other people's opinions. It's the belief that you are not deserving of having the relationship you want, simply because it never worked out before or someone told you it won't. The foundation is immersed in the feeling of lack, whether this is a lack of self-worth, self-love, self-confidence, or even a lack of perspective of one's infinite potential.

This is one of the most negative perspectives you can have of yourself. It goes against everything I've ever taught. **Feeling unworthy is the result of you not tapping into your infinite nature and instead, playing the victim role.** Let's break down this feeling and how to break free from it once and for all.

How It Comes About

So many of us feel unworthy that it might as well be declared as a global issue. It comes about from past experiences in life and past results.

Our parents, our educational system, and society compare us to one another from the perspective that we are not good enough until we prove our worthiness. We are compared, judged, and ranked according to when our developmental milestones are reached as children, how well we do in school, how much we are liked, how much we've accomplished, and how well connected we are socially. Unless you have been an over-achiever in everything you have ever tried, you will feel the sting of comparison and competition, hence, the disparaging feeling of not being worthy.

In other words, unworthiness comes from defining your value based on the external conditions and expectations that physical reality places on you. Accepting other people's judgment and allowing their judgment to make you feel 'less than' is common amongst peer groups. When you identify yourself with the limitation of ideas, labels, and moments from the past, you're defining yourself based on concepts that technically do not exist. The only real truth is your own. Here. Now.

How to Fix It

When you start to understand that you were born worthy and have nothing to prove, you will start to feel worthy enough to overcome any feelings of unworthiness. Understandably, you may feel skeptical about this. How can you suddenly start to believe this, if you haven't your entire life?

Start to see yourself from the perspective of source energy. Many spiritual teachers teach us that we are actually eternal beings of consciousness, and that we never die. That should be enough to empower you, but there's so much more to it.

Every single thing you want (created from the contrast you've experienced and the resultant understanding of what you don't want), has been shot out into the universe like a rocket. Your creation of desire is now in turn helping the universe to expand. **In other words, YOU are helping to expand the universe with your desires, no matter how small, or how big**. You *are* worthy of having your desires met. You were born worthy.

Recognize you are worthy by default. When you remove all the stories, filters, and limiting beliefs, you're left with the greatest version of you: an infinite and ever-expanding spiritual being that's connected to all the magic in the cosmos. You have limitless potential and radiate magnetism like no other when you're being your true self.

Once you embrace this, you'll never feel unworthy again.

TECHNIQUE #5: HABIT OF THOUGHT MEDITATION

The Habit of Thought Meditation technique is meant to bring awareness around the thinking habits you have going on inside of your head. Without judging or labeling these thoughts, we're going to shed a light on them and identify whether these are thoughts that are or are not in alignment with the best version of you. Shifting away from old trains of thought will help you become more accustomed to a new way of being.

Follow the steps I've outlined below. This meditation can take as long as you'd like:

Step 1: Find a comfortable and quiet place to sit or lay down.

Step 2: Take a couple of deep breaths and focus your awareness on your breathing.

Step 3: After feeling like you've entered the present moment, consider imagining a situation that is uncomfortable for you. Think of an unknown reality that you're afraid of stepping into. This can be a new relationship with someone, a situation in a current relationship, or even a situation you've experienced in the past and you are afraid of experiencing again. Don't stay too caught up in this step. Avoid identifying with this situation and labeling it as something negative or specific to you. Keep it general and broad.

Step 4: Notice all of the thoughts that arise from this situation. What kind of limiting beliefs are you creating for yourself? What circumstance in the past is influencing your decision in this situation? How do you think or feel about yourself in this situation? Bring awareness to all of this fear, anxiety, and insecurity that have been hidden in your subconscious.

Step 5: Choose to experience this reality differently. Play out the situation in your mind, and respond to it accordingly with your new set of beliefs. How do you want to position yourself in this situation? What is the outcome of you stepping into this new identity? How do you feel as a result of this? Embody the confidence, love, security, appreciation, stability, wholeness, and presence that come with this new version of you.

Step 6: Take one last deep breath and journal your experience from steps 3-5. What was the situation you thought of? What were the first thoughts that came to mind? How did you respond differently with your new identity? After this meditation, you should feel, even if only slightly, more open and less anxious about the situation.

Step 7: Express gratitude for every single session.

Consider doing this on a daily basis until every uncomfortable imagined reality in your mind is no longer uncomfortable. Find comfort in the unknown. This will help you respond proactively to your environment and put you in a state that is more aligned with your true self and desires.

"When you fish for love, bait with your heart, not your brain."

– Mark Twain

CHAPTER 4

Two Types of Love and Where to Place Your Focus

One of the most overlooked topics, when it comes to love, is whether it is conditional, or unconditional. What do you think? Is this a choice, or something beyond our control?

Do you love someone because of what they can give you (conditional)? Or do you love them no matter what they do (unconditional)? But isn't it bad to love someone unconditionally, like the people pleaser who, on the surface, loves people unconditionally? Where do you draw the line? What is the line? And who gets to draw it?

These probing questions will help you to clarify the topic of love, self-awareness, the power of choice, and how to paradoxically shift your focus towards yourself in a way that allows you to exude your magnetic nature, and thus, attract an amazing relationship.

First, we need to understand what conditional versus un-conditional love really means. A good way to generally look at the difference between these two forms of love is to compare the love from a mother to that of a father. A mother's love, typically, is unconditional. Your mother will love you no matter what you do. But a father's love, again, typically, is more conditional. The father's love is given only after the child has performed well (a condition) or to his liking. This is of course an extremely generalized observation, with not every mother or father being like this. Most of us however, can more easily understand the difference between conditional and unconditional love when we consider the mother/father comparison.

CONDITIONAL LOVE

Conditional love is love that relies on certain external conditions. In computer programming, it's the "IF (blank) THEN (blank) ELSE (condition)" statement. In life, this is applied as, "IF (this person does what I want), THEN (I will love them) ELSE (I will not)."

This kind of love can often be tied to controlling and manipulative behaviors. In most cases, the one who practices conditional love believes they can control others, and if others cannot be controlled, then they should not be loved.

Conditional love is defined by the ego, the state where, as Dr. Wayne Dyer used to say, we "Edge God Out." When we edge God or source energy out of our lives, we replace our normal, natural, divinely inspired unconditional state with conditional love. But who you really are is infinite source energy in physical form. Anything that has conditions, limitations, or constraints is coming from a false sense of self.

Conditional love is love that does not express one's true feelings for the other. It is love that feels stuck, limited, resistant, and sometimes uncomfortable. Conditional love can often be rooted in these lower vibrational frequencies which can affect other aspects of your life.

In addition, it can be based on the condition of whether or not the other person feels love too. If they love you, then you love them. If they don't love you, then you don't love them. Conditional love considers what other people think, what other people do, who they are, how much money they make, how attractive they are, how they treat themselves, how they treat others, their upbringing, their socioeconomic standing, and many other factors. It's no wonder it's so hard to find a loving relationship when you're looking at it from these perspectives. Most people only operate in the conditional love arena of life where everything about the person is scrutinized, judged, and compared.

Loving in this way drains energy from both people, and it sets up distrust and suspicion. You may feel that things are going well now, but might have constant concerns about the future. What if he or she looks at another person with lust in their heart? What then? Should I leave them? Where do I draw the line?

Where *do* you draw the line?

Conditional love is all about line drawing. But isn't setting standards of how you want to be treated important? The answer is yes. There is a difference between being conditional and setting healthy boundaries, which we will discuss shortly.

Conditional love fills a void in a person, which should not have been there to begin with. Remember, you were born whole.

You *are* whole. If you feel you need someone to fill a void of loneliness within your heart, then you'll keep on attracting more loneliness, or relationships that cycle that emotion. This type of love is based more on the superficial representation of the relationship then on the actual relationship. Many times, this manifests in the form of a couple who do not have any chemistry, and do not even really like one another, but remain together out of convenience, financial gain, or social status. This kind of love causes all kinds of heartache and pain within a relationship.

When people require conditions in order to feel love, it goes against the laws of true manifestation. In other words, in the conditional love mindset, love cannot be expressed without conditions. This is the opposite of manifestation.

UNCONDITIONAL LOVE

Unconditional love, on the other hand, is independent from any external conditions. It is a way of being, rather than a way of acting. It is an internal mindset, not an external construct. It is love that is defined by your inner being – that all knowing part of you who knows the value of every person on planet Earth.

It is love that comes from your true self – love that expresses your true feelings for the other from a place of non-judgment, compassion, forgiveness, and understanding. It is love that sees the best in others, whether they deserve it or not. As the Bible says, love, or unconditional love, "bears all things, believes all things, hopes all things, and endures all things."

It is love that feels free, is limitless, flows easily, and is comfortable. It gives without expecting anything in return because it knows and understands that the gift of giving is the reward in itself. It is love that builds up energy in both people, rather than detracting it. It is love that makes your partner feel the blessed breath of freedom, while at the same time, causing them to love you even more.

This type of love encourages partners to feel empowered about themselves, instead of worrying about each other. It complements the other's desired frequency, yet isn't dependent upon it – it is love that allows the other to be complete within themselves, without judgment.

This kind of love allows the other person to be who they want to be, regardless of what that is. The problem in most relationships is that partners start to grow apart because they never honestly gave each other the freedom to grow into whoever they were becoming. And then, one day, they wake up and think their partner isn't the same person they married. Conditional love would be disappointed with that. Unconditional love would be perfectly fine.

Unconditional love allows for growth, expansion, and even retraction, and hard times. It loves no matter what the person is going through – whether that be financially difficult times, a dark night of the soul experience, or other temporary problems. This kind of love does not keep track of past negative events or experiences. It doesn't remind your partner of the wrongs they have done.

As mentioned above with regards to conditional love, people require conditions in order to feel love, resulting in the opposite of manifestation. Unconditional love on the other hand, *creates* conditions. That is true manifestation.

> *"Love can only be found through the act of loving."*
> – Paulo Coelho

UNCONDITIONALLY LOVING YOURSELF

This is probably one of the most difficult concepts to understand and much of it depends upon your own spiritual advancement on the emotional scale to true love, freedom, peace, and joy.

Self-love is about giving yourself what you need in the form of self-care, to enable you to unconditionally love others, while still being considerate and compromising in situations which do not overstep your boundaries. It is an important part of what affects the vibrational frequency you emit.

Self-absorption, on the other hand, does emit the energy of arrogance or superiority over others. You can tell the difference relatively easily, as self-absorption reflects as a lack of consideration or ability to compromise. And this usually happens because of one's inability to be vulnerable or open when it comes to expressing their weaknesses. When it comes to finding the right balance, defining your values and constructing boundaries can be a big help.

With that being said, no one can tell you to create boundaries or not – or where to set them. That is totally up to you. In other words, no one can tell you how far to take the concept of unconditional love. To make the point really clear so it's easily understood, total unconditional love with a partner would not necessarily enforce monogamy. But if you had a partner who truly loved you and felt the same way you did, they would never venture outside of the relationship. When people are given the freedom to be truly free in a relationship, the opposite of what you think usually happens. In many cases, that kind of freedom will make them love you even more, and give them even less reason to venture outside of the relationship.

Unconditional love may seem like it would attract abusers and people who would take advantage of you. It cannot happen if you are truly unconditionally loving to yourself and others. This is because you would not tolerate consistently reoccurring negative behaviors in a relationship, knowing that it is detrimental not just to you, but both people. You would also only attract those who would vibrationally match you in those high-flying feelings of love, joy, and freedom. When you are unconditionally loving, the perspective of being taken advantage of should never cross your mind, because you didn't partake in the act of giving with the expectation of receiving anything in return. You gave because it felt good and in alignment with your inner being.

Honor your intuitive instinct. Respect your gut feeling on relationships and people. Don't let any book, mentor, or guru tell you what is right for you – only you know. Having said all this, can you turn around any relationships with true unconditional love? The answer is yes, you can. But if you are not consistently honoring your truth and setting the right boundaries, these relationships will continue to drag you down rather than match or lift you to the life you want to live.

But here is the one piece of advice that you must always adhere to…

Always, always, *always*, unconditionally love yourself first before anyone else. Be patient with yourself. Eat healthy foods so that your energy and mood are positively affected. Improve on your sleeping habits. Create boundaries and take some time out to process, unwind and pray or meditate. Follow your highest excitement and curiosity. All of these things are a choice. All of those 'reasons' currently running through your head of why you can't do these things – question them. In all likelihood, they are mere excuses, not reasons. And excuses are easier to overcome than reasons… because overcoming them has nothing to do with what's outside of you. All the power you need can be found within.

THE POWER OF SELF-AWARENESS AND CHOICE

To be aware of self and to become aware of awareness itself, is the act of seeing yourself through the eyes of source. The power of self-awareness gives us the opportunity to place our focus wherever we choose.

This is the first step to shifting from the low vibration that comes with conditional living, into a higher one. This paves the way to more quickly and easily expand into who you really are, and as a result, increases the probability of you attracting love into your life.

You need to know that if you are too focused on how you've failed in past relationships, how nothing is working out for you, or how you might not find anyone in the future; then you are creating the destiny that you do not prefer through the conditions you've set for yourself. Avoid *reacting* emotionally to any situation and choose to *respond* to negative emotion through self-awareness. If you're unaware of where you're placing your focus, you're manifesting by chance and not through choice. This means you could manifest the same old type of relationships you've always been attracting, and its resulting misery.

Become aware of yourself, your own actions, and who you *really* are, so that you can then manifest the relationship you truly desire. Choose to focus on the potential you have to attract a positive relationship, on the essence of why a relationship is something important to you, on what you will get out of this relationship, and on how it will make you feel. Place your focus on the right things, notice your vibration reflect it, and as a result, the happening of the manifestation of your desire.

When you develop the practice of self-awareness, you naturally choose to think better feeling thoughts. You become more optimistic, and you are more aware of the subtle positive aspects of your life. Instead of trying to fight the frequency of lack, you're moving into the frequency of abundance.

Once you've had a taste of the frequency of love, using the power of self-awareness, you can consciously tune yourself into this frequency whenever you want. Your day-to-day will normally bring up conditioned thoughts and patterns. It's important that you recognize conditions, labels, and definitions as subjective or illusionary. When you do this, you vibrationally detach yourself from these traps. The goal is simple. **Detach from the frequency of your situation and embody the frequency of your visualization.**

SHIFT YOUR FOCUS INSIDE

The key to attracting and finding the best relationship is when you realize you can create all of the feelings of having that relationship *without actually having one.*

Is that a paradigm shift of understanding for you? You've always had the power to create the feeling first. Most of us would balk at that statement. Most of us would say, "That can't be! I had a relationship where I felt like I was walking on cloud 9 and I could never create that on my own!"

You may think that's true, but it's not. You are the one who chooses to feel anything – there isn't anyone outside of you who creates it – it's all you. When you fully understand this, then you can take all of your power back, and control over your thoughts and emotions.

Every single one of your relationships is a reflection of you. If you are in a poor mental and emotional state, this will reflect in how you interact with others, how others interact with you, and who you attract into your life.

Every feeling, sensation, and love you ever want to feel can come from within. A high vibration does not need to come from your relationships, partners, or other people (conditions). Your focus should constantly be on your choice to feel however you want to feel despite what's being portrayed in your physical reality.

Another reason why this is so important is because attachment to things outside of your control *will* deplete your energy. When you place excess importance or dependency on factors outside of you, you give all of your power away. As a result, you create resistance towards what you want and move yourself out of balance. The expression 'Where your focus goes, energy flows' illustrates this perfectly. If you're attaching your energy to factors outside of you, where will all the energy you need to create go? How will you become magnetic if you don't have any magnetic energy to emit?

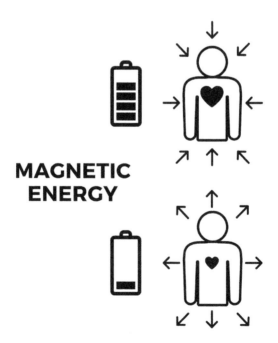

MAGNETIC ENERGY

Create reasons to feel good, even if it doesn't make sense to your rational mind. Even if you're living through the worst time in your life, you have the choice to align yourself with who you really are deep inside. If there are plenty of reasons outside of you to feel grateful, appreciative, and loving, that's amazing. If there are no reasons, that's okay too. Because you always have your own imagination and internal creations there to support you. **There's always a way to raise your vibration.**

Your focus determines your vibration. Focus on possibility, abundance, and how your desires make you feel and why you enjoy them so much. When you shift your focus to what is happening internally, instead of externally, then you will create what you want externally – *that's* manifestation in action.

TECHNIQUE #6: SELF-IMAGE REFLECTION

Using this technique, you're going to be answering the following questions about yourself in a journal, to help shed a light on:

- all of the positive, strong, and magnetic traits that you possess
- letting go of old beliefs that do not serve you anymore

Often times, we're overshadowed by all the negative and bad things we've been carrying with us throughout our lives. With this reflection technique, we're going to be bringing everything up to the surface. After doing this exercise, consider reading the answers to yourself every single day until you've embodied this new way of being.

1. Write down the five things you love most about yourself in this exact moment in time.
2. Recall a time when you felt like you were embodying the best version of yourself. Describe in detail how it felt or feels like to be confident, open, expansive, magnetic, secure, whole, grateful, appreciative, stable, aligned, loved, excited, fun, sensual, and alive. Write about the three to five words that resonated with you the most.
3. Create a list of your five greatest strengths and traits. Ignore how other people have reacted to these in the past and write down what feels authentic to *you*.
4. List your five greatest challenges in life and write down exactly how you overcame them or how you intend to overcome them.

5. Write down the five greatest lessons that you've learned from all the challenges that life threw at you. Describe how important these lessons will be for you in the future and how they have helped you grow as a person.

6. Write a forgiveness letter to others that have done you wrong and to yourself. Express it in a way that feels like you're letting go of it for good. Keep these for yourself if you prefer but giving them to the person is often a much more powerful and transformational experience, especially if this is someone you were/are really close to.

7. Describe in detail the new identity you want to step into. Write down the core values, beliefs, and expectations for yourself that you will embody.

8. Write down the boundaries that you will set for yourself in order to align with this new identity. Describe in detail what you will not tolerate and put up with anymore.

9. Describe in your own words what it means to be in love.

TECHNIQUE #7: EMOTIONAL EVIDENCE BASED BELIEF

In the process of attracting a loving relationship, you may find it difficult to stay optimistic given the lack of the physical manifestation of it. This is evidence that shows you are building a faulty belief system due to your object of focus.

When you use external reality as a confirmation to whether you should believe something or not, then you are shutting down the infinite possibilities that can present themselves to you. When your focus is on what you have (in this case, the lack of a loving relationship), you'll continue to manifest more of it.

In order to break free from this cycle, use the Emotional Evidence Based Belief technique by looking for confirmation within. The previous technique (Self Image Reflection) can also assist in this process. **In other words, use your positive emotional state as the confirmation that you are getting into alignment with what you want to attract**. If you are feeling secure, loved, appreciated, and whole, *without* the physical manifestation of your desired relationship, that is *all* the confirmation you need to know that *what you want is on its way*. This is how you build the belief system that shapes your identity, and as a result, shapes your reality.

Recognize your alignment and confirm that this is what you've been looking for. Appreciate these moments and the universe will inevitably start moving pieces around to create synchronicities that match this new frequency.

"*I am not what happened to me, I am what I choose to become.*"

— Carl Jung

C H A P T E R   5

Embodying Magnetism: Authentic Charisma

Have you ever noticed how magnetic someone with charisma is, seemingly easily attracting whatever it is they want to themselves? And have you ever wondered how they developed that charisma? Is it something anyone can develop? Or is it something you have to be born with?

The good news is that *anyone* can develop it when you fully understand what it is and what is at the heart of it. Anyone can learn to become more charismatic, which will make it much easier to attract the relationships you desire. In this chapter, we will take a look at breaking free from your false identity, owning who you are, and becoming the person you want to become.

First, let's cover 3 topics in order to gain clarity around the subject...

WHAT IS YOUR FALSE IDENTITY?

Awareness of having a problem is 90% of the solution. When you become aware of your false identity (we all have it), then you're almost there…

Have you ever met someone, dated them for a while, and everything was going well, but then as soon as it got more serious, things started to change? Maybe they were the 'perfect match' throughout the dating period, but once the relationship reached the point where it was committed, both of you started to show your true colors. In this kind of a relationship, you start off acting from the ego, then as time goes on, it reaches a stage where you can no longer hide your shortcomings and vulnerability, and before you know it, the chemistry disappears.

It's a very common experience. To a degree, we all do it by being on our best behavior during the courting phase of any relationship. The point is that taking on a false identity can be a conscious decision that someone makes… but what if it's unconscious?

Most of us have developed false identities that are based upon our ego's attachment to past relationships, experiences, and ideas. The ego works hard to convince us that who we are is the result of all of the external things that we experience and how we perceive them. It makes us feel stagnant and stuck. For example, if we fail in one subject matter in school, then the automatic conclusion is that we are a failure at that subject. If we excel, then we are successful. The ego will come to conclusions based upon our limited view of the world, and has a difficult time accepting that anything else can be true. This is why if someone believes that all men are bad, they will not be open to any reality where some men are good.

Our ego regrets the past, is worried about the future, and never lives in the present moment. This is why it has such a strong desire to control, instead of to let go. It is a relentless cog in the wheel of our life that doesn't want us to experience the here and now – the present moment. The basic motive of the ego is to protect us, but its reasoning ability comes from a very basic, reptilian part of our brain that cannot connect with higher levels of intelligence. The ego is the animal part of our brain that is fearful, defensive, limited, and unconscious. It is your mind's voice of doubt. It is the voice that tells you to not try anything for fear of how you will look to others. It is the voice that tells you to play it safe. The ego is defensive, and often times will cause certain people to repel from you.

The ego places a very high value on external things and experiences – things that we've become attached to and use to define us through our memory, thus keeping us stuck in a certain way of thinking. **This analysis of our external life experiences creates our false identity – the false self.** This false self may tell you that you don't deserve love, or that it'll never work out. It wants you to stay attached to an identity that's been confirmed externally from past experiences. This could be due to your unconscious choice to experience those moments the way you did over and over again.

When you realize that your ego is *not* your true self, you can start to let go of the old you and embrace the new, limitless you. When you become aware of your false identity, then you can start to create a new reality – a reality that sets you up to develop charisma that makes you magnetic to exactly the kind of relationship you want to attract. We'll talk more about this in a later section.

WE ARE ETERNAL SPIRITUAL BEINGS

All of us are living in a temporary, human experience. Your physical experience is temporary, but your nonphysical experience is eternal. Therefore, there is no reason to stay attached to one way of being. You can become anyone you wish to become, whenever you want. It may take some time to grasp this, or even to apply it, but just so you know, it's not impossible.

All it takes is to let go of the expectations and judgments coming from the outside world, as well as renegotiating certain energetic agreements you've made with people in your life. In other words, if you want to be a better and more magnetic version of yourself, you need to be open to detaching from your old non-magnetic identity. Thinking, feeling, and acting differently is required if you want to experience a new reality. It all starts from within.

When you realize that you are an eternal being, it should warm your heart knowing that this life is not all there is, and that you'll never stop expanding. You are a powerful, ever-expanding, forever growing being who will never stop desiring new things. When you fully understand who you really are, all worry, doubt, and fear will melt away. It is our ego's desire to stay attached to an identity that keeps us in the mindset of lack, limitation, worry, and fear. But when you become aware, and decide to let go, you free yourself from its constraints.

Understanding this core belief that we have a *never-changing* nature will allow you to see beyond what you think is true.

WHAT TO EXPECT WITH CHANGE

To the ego, any kind of change is a threat to the status quo, and could be threatening and dangerous. Since most people live from the ego state of mind, you can expect with high certainty that they are going to test this new identity you're building for yourself.

Although you do get what you expect to get, don't be surprised if people react differently to this new version of you. Don't be surprised if they judge and give their opinion. Go easy on yourself during this time of transformation and change. Expect yourself to yo-yo back and forth between the new way and old way of being until you've completely transformed. Transformation takes time. Others won't like it. Be prepared.

This new way of being will attract new life experiences that you otherwise wouldn't have had. It may be uncomfortable at first, but realize that these new experiences are exactly what you were asking for with this new identity you've embodied. They are coming from the unknown, and that is why it might feel uncomfortable and unexpected.

This is your manifestation. This is usually when your ego will try and pull you back to the old way of thinking and try to convince you that there is something wrong with what you're experiencing. Be aware of these thoughts so that you can then shine a light on them, thus giving them less power over you.

BEING 'AS IF'

Remember the Law of Attraction concept to 'act as if it already happened?' The idea is to take about 5 minutes a day to get quiet, close your eyes, and visualize from the first-person perspective of whatever it is that you want. The promise was that if you could visualize every detail of what you wanted, then you could raise your vibration to what it would feel like, and as a result, you would attract it.

The only problem is that it takes much more time than just 5 minutes. The new solution is to memorize the feeling you created during the practice and take it with you into the rest of your day. When you can embody this version 2.0 of you all day long instead of just for 5 minutes, then you will accelerate the manifestation of whatever desire it is you want.

This is why your goal should be to go from 'acting as if' to 'being as if'. In other words, don't just pretend what you want is here, live it. What is the difference? And how do you distinguish between the two? Take the current dating landscape as an example. Say a man spends money on a car he cannot afford, talks about things he knows nothing about, and goes against his own values just to impress others. This is how you 'act as if.' In other words, it's faking it, until you make it.

But what if we were to flip the equation around? Say a man spends money on his own self-education, studies more about a subject he wants to learn about, and sticks to his values no matter what, in order to attract only the right kind of people. This is how you 'be as if.' In other words, it's making it, until you make it. This is the idea of building your own self-worth.

When you behave from a superficial level, you do indeed tune into a frequency that radiates a sense of self-worth. It is true that if you fake it, you can actually make it. But be warned: reality *will* test you. Things will show up where you need to actually be the part, and not just play it. Actors in movies act the part, but when the scene is over, they go back to being who they really are. The act is only for show. This same idea applies in life. This is the reason why a relationship can end so quickly. You enter it with a false identity, and slowly start to show your real colors as time goes on, because the mask is starting to slip off.

If you want to make real change happen, you need to focus on the change that is happening internally and not externally. Buying flashy accessories will not make you more magnetic. It'll only superficially and temporarily cover up the truth; the expression of your true self. Create desire for someone to be attracted to you. Bring energetic value to the table by giving other's permission to be themselves. Giving, when it comes from the heart, is an action that is inviting and energetically positive.

Building your own sense of self-worth is far more sustainable than 'acting as if' because it doesn't depend on conditions. It is work that starts from the inside, thus radiating an energy that is more dense, sustainable, and unshakeable when faced with challenges and contrast.

Be the person that would attract other people into their circle based upon who they truly are and what they truly want. Express your truth with no filters because it's the most magnetic identity you can embody. It's the identity that feels natural, flowing, and in alignment with your deepest desires, including a romantic relationship that lasts.

This process goes far beyond embodying the experience of being in a relationship. When you choose to create your own self-worth, you're embodying the person in the relationship. Notice the subtle shift. Even though visualizing the *experience* is a step in the right direction, embodying the *person* that is in the experience is even more powerful.

THE KEY TO MAGNETISM AND CHARISMA

Do not be afraid of making the first move if you feel called to. In other words, do not be afraid of embodying the confident and charismatic you when your intuition is guiding you there. When you overcome the fears you have related to social interactions and romantic relationships, you naturally and energetically radiate a new energy that allows you to step into a new vibrational reality for yourself. Whether taking this step works in your favor or not physically, non-physical, you've already sent out a new signal.

The moment you give yourself the freedom to be yourself (whoever you truly want to be); the more magnetic you are to others. Why? Because when you're being yourself, you're living in alignment with your inner being, which is naturally very magnetic and charismatic. When you live life from the eyes of source energy - from your inner being's perspective - you are a joyful, happy, passionate, eager, magnetic, and authentically charismatic person.

Everyone is naturally magnetic. All it takes is to remove the egoic filters that have been created through the external lens of judgment and comparison. When you're operating from a high vibrational state, you're operating from a magnetic state. When you're at a high vibrational frequency, you attract people that also have the intention of living at a high vibrational frequency. In this case, like attracts like.

> *"Love is not something that is a sort of rare commodity, everyone has it."*

> **– Alan Watts**

This high vibrational frequency feels loose, easy, effortless, fun, exciting, and worry-free - not needy, contrived, desperate, or insecure. When you embody this high vibrational version of you, you give permission for others to be themselves. You become more approachable. You will instantly light up any room that you walk into, and raise the vibration of everyone around you.

When you're open like this, you invite the unknown into your life. You surrender to the spontaneity of the universe. When you embody this magnetic energy, it's easy to give up the vibration of neediness because energetically, you have everything you need.

Own who you are. Be the true you. And watch how quickly the relationship you desire manifests in your life.

TECHNIQUE #8: ENERGETIC STRETCHING AND DANCING

For this technique, we're going to be moving your focus from your heart and mind into your body. Personal magnetism doesn't only involve thinking and feeling a certain way. Our bodies are the vehicle at which we radiate magnetic energy to the outside world. So understanding how to express yourself physically is essential if you want to truly embody magnetism.

The same way you do weight training or cardio to change your physical body, this technique will help change how you personally feel about your body on an energetic level. This is also a powerful way of allowing your body to release tension from traumas and wounds that are still lingering inside of you. The difference in energy between having a straight back and a slouching one is only one of the more obvious examples of this. This technique can be described in two words: Ecstatic Movement

Whether you're dancing or stretching, giving your body the freedom to move in a way that is purely intuitive is an excellent way to open up your energy. Dancing and stretching as a form of release is nothing new. Consider yoga, a practice that has been around for thousands of years, as a form of ecstatic movement. You don't need to attend ecstatic dance clubs to get the full effects of this. A simple 3-5 minute intuitive stretching sessions every morning at home is enough. Give room for your body to express itself naturally every once in a while. Not only will this help open up your energy, but it'll get you feeling more comfortable about yourself, thus, bringing about a new sense of authentic confidence and charisma.

Here are seven tips to get the most out of your ecstatic movement session:

1. Focus on intuition and moving with the flow of your body. Let go of all conscious decision making.
2. Breathe into your belly and not your chest before initiating the movement. Try your best not to hold your breath.
3. Keep your awareness on the sensations of your body. Stay grounded and present.
4. Allow your shoulders to relax and keep your sternum up during certain movements.
5. Pull your spine up at the solar plexus so it stays open and not slouched.
6. Avoid energy stagnation by not staying still for too long.
7. When you have thoughts, check in with how the body is feeling at the exact moment they arise.

Throughout your session, be conscious about the energy that you give off. Be in tune with your thoughts and feelings. Relax.

TECHNIQUE #9: SELF-FULFILLING QUESTIONS

This technique derives from the self-fulfilling prophecy theory. This theory states that an original expectation leads to its own confirmation. In other words, if you're expecting something to happen to you, then it will. For this technique, we're going to be revamping your self-fulfilling prophecy by asking yourself questions that confirm the expectations that you have. This is a way of confirming your expectation before they manifest.

For example, let's say you label yourself as a shy and anxious person. Hence, whenever you go on a date or meet new people, they will catch onto this belief because you've already labeled yourself as a shy and anxious person. As a result, that is going to be your state of being as you radiate the energy associated with those beliefs. A new belief takes time to solidify because it can only be strengthened by confirmation. We often only depend on external confirmation, which is why new beliefs hardly ever stick. For this technique, you're going to be confirming these new beliefs internally by asking yourself questions. These questions will imply that your new identity is already solidified before it's been confirmed externally.

Here are a few examples of questions you can start asking yourself. I encourage you to create your own questions too. This will help you get into the mood of asking yourself questions that raise your vibration at any time and place:

When being single:
- Why do I feel so whole and complete?
- Why am I so in love with myself?
- Why is my relationship with myself so healthy?
- Why do I love spending time with myself?
- Why am I excited about who I'm attracting?

When going out to social events:
- Why am I talking to people so confidently?
- Why am I attracting positive attention from other people?
- Why am I so open and engaging in new social interactions?

When being on a date:
- What part of this date is fun for me?
- What interests me about this person?
- How am I handling this date so well?
- Where did this confidence of mine come from?
- Why am I so happy about this moment?

When being in a relationship:
- What makes me happy about this relationship?
- What do I love about my partner?
- Why do I feel loved, appreciated, and secure?
- What makes this person so fun to be around?

"Love is an untamed force. When we try to control it, it destroys us. When we try to imprison it, it enslaves us. When we try to understand it, it leaves us feeling lost and confused."

– Paul Coelho

CHAPTER 6

Easy Loving: The Path of Least Resistance and Most Love

Now that you know more about how magnetic energy works, we can talk about easy loving, what the path of least resistance is, and the path to experiencing the most love possible in your life. We're going to talk about how important it is to have a high vibration in all aspects of your life and how following your passions outside of relationships will actually help you attract more, better quality, relationships.

Most people struggle with their ego and don't allow love to encapsulate every aspect of their lives. The struggle is internal, but once you understand what it is, then you can begin to let go and let yourself be guided towards the path of least resistance or most allowance and most love.

Before you began reading this book, you may have thought that finding your soul mate involved something outside of yourself – it was a quest – a search – something that you had to find. But the best way to search for love is to create the love you want inside of yourself first, and then in all areas of your life before you 'search' for anyone. After creating love for yourself in all aspects of your life, searching for that perfect relationship isn't even necessary because they will come into your life naturally. When it happens, it will feel easy, fun, light, and exciting. You won't have to play games because this time you got the universe to do the hard work of searching for the perfect match. This method is a much different way of going about manifesting the love of your life because it leverages your state of being over anything else.

This can seem like a more time-consuming method, but in reality, it only further reinforces what we've already talked about in previous chapters. When you can embody your best self, you can attract the best relationship for you. It's simply a matter of consistently building up the natural magnetism that is already inside of you.

Love yourself so thoroughly and completely that you are just oozing love, confidence, happiness, fun, appreciation, and respect for yourself and others. Be easy on yourself when it comes to manifesting love. And create it in every aspect of your life so that your love vibration is revving and humming along, repelling anyone who isn't a vibrational match.

Don't go out there in a desperate frame of mind and decide that you're going to help someone to raise their vibration to match yours. That's asking for trouble. Instead, set your standards high, and keep them there. Rather than lower your high standards, know that the right person will be attracted to your unique energetic signature.

VIBRATION MIGRATION

When you understand why and how vibration migration works, you'll understand exactly why you've been getting what you've been getting in life. You see, the universe doesn't care what topic you think about – all it cares about is what frequency you emit. In other words, everything could be going great in your life – your health, your wealth, and your relationships too. However, if you focus on even just one thing that is going wrong in your life for too long, it becomes prominent in your vibration. This lowers your vibration in ALL other aspects of your life too.

How you do one thing is how you do everything... let me explain.

If you loathe your job, despise the type of work you do, and wake up every morning dreading to start the day, this vibration will carry over to your relationships. If this work is something you do 5 times a week, and 8 hours a day, that means you're in a low vibration for a very long time. It will become your normal vibration if you focus on it too much for too long. In this state, it's impossible to become a magnet to love when the frequency you're radiating is that of hate, boredom, and lack of fulfillment. Even worse, if you do attract someone while you are in a low vibration, they will match your low vibration, inevitably leading to a problematic relationship. Changing your current job or career can be a massive leap that not many people are willing to take. There are ways to get around this however, and that's by changing how you view the work you do. Changing the meaning of what you do, where you go, and how you do your work, is an excellent first step to making the vibrational shift.

It doesn't matter what you allow to lower your vibration. If you choose to allow anything to get you upset or down for too long, everything in your life will snowball and become a problem too. This is where the expression, 'When it rains, it pours' comes from. When you focus too much on the negatives of your life, more negatives will come.

The goal should be to carry a high vibration in everything you do, no matter if it has to do with your relationships or not. This is key to defining your **default frequency** as one that matches with your desired reality.

You'll often get pushed out of alignment, but that's okay. There is a buffer of time before things manifest, so don't beat yourself up or worry if you find yourself getting momentarily upset, frustrated, or angry. Simply do not attach your sense of self to these states of being. Do not get caught up. As long as you keep your focus on what makes you feel good in the moment and allow yourself to be the version of you that's in the frequency of love, that's all that matters to the universe.

Do things that raise your vibration. What this means from a practical perspective is to be good to yourself more often. Go to the beach. Get a massage. Eat out at your favorite restaurant. Call a good friend. Rent a bunch of 'feel good' movies and watch them. Go for a walk, hike, or bike. Nourish yourself well with healthy foods and snacks. Get plenty of sleep. Say 'no' more often to others when it feels right – which essentially means saying 'yes' to *you* more often. Embrace being what you normally would consider to be a little selfish, but this time, do it with no guilt. Remember – there is a big difference between being self-absorbed and practicing self-love. Self-love is good!

There is nothing more important, for both you and those around you, than you feeling your best. That means choosing to feel good under any and all circumstances. Note, this does not mean to follow what is familiar to you. Familiarity, often times, isn't exciting, and it doesn't feed your curiosity. This is a trap many people easily fall into, so keep this in mind. I know all of these concepts are hard to believe because you've probably been taught that you have to "face reality."

But instead of "facing reality," *create* it! Yes - create it yourself! That's how the universe works anyway. You create your reality by choosing which one you want to live. Take a step back, be the observer, and choose which thoughts and emotions you want to resonate with the most. Do not get too attached, because attachment to anything, good or bad, creates resistance. Remember, you are infinite. You are so much more than what you stay stuck in or limit yourself to. Get yourself on the path of least resistance to the best relationship of your life, but more importantly, to the best relationship with yourself.

FOLLOW YOUR PASSION AND PURPOSE

"Follow your bliss" Joseph Campbell once so aptly put it. Find your passion. Discover your purpose. **Let the relationship be the side effect of you living your best life independently.** Become whole yourself so you can attract a whole person. Become the person you want to attract by putting yourself first in your life.

This is powerful because it removes the vibration of *wanting* and shifts you into the vibration of *having*. This opens you up to attracting relationships that are deeper, more passionate, and more fulfilling because they're in alignment with what you're doing every day.

Don't ever try to become what you think someone else wants or needs you to become. In the end, you'll be out of alignment. You'll feel resistance instantly because your state of being will not come from a place of authentic truth. It'll come from external conditioning. This not only leads to more struggle when it comes to manifesting your dream relationship, but it'll also leave you unhappy and unfulfilled with the ones you do attract. The best way to attract your envisioned ideal person into your life is to fall in love with yourself *and* your own life.

As you work on yourself, your natural glow will start to shine through in everything you do. You'll find it easier to be guided by your intuition. Decisions will start leading to spontaneous encounters that you never would have imagined. People and circumstances will start showing up in your life like never before. All you need to do is ride your own wave, and let the water take you to where you truly want to go. You attract to you based on who you are being, and if you get yourself to your best version in other areas of your life, you'll find it easier to attract someone that will want to be a part of that too.

THE LAW OF DETACHMENT

The Law of Detachment is the act of surrendering to the divine. It's the act of following the path of least resistance, which simply means to make choices that feel good and in alignment with who you want to be at any given moment in time. It's having full confidence, trust, and faith that your desired relationship will manifest itself instead of labelling the possibility of it with an idea, limitation, opinion, or external condition.

If you're attached, you radiate signals of doubt and distrust. Be exclusively loyal to your intuition. This is the path to a fulfilling and love-filled life. Contrary to popular belief, this does not mean you do not care. It means you care, and a lot more than most people can see on the surface level. **Honoring your truth is your greatest service to others.** And when it comes to relationships, this is how you attract and manifest the best of the best.

ATTACHMENT	DETACHMENT
RESISTANCE	FLOW
STUCKNESS	FREEDOM
NEEDINESS	HAVINGNESS
LACKING	ABUNDANT
FINITE	INFINITE
CONTROLLING	ALLOWING
MANIPULATIVE	MAGNETIC
ANXIOUS	TRUSTING

Here are the 3 most common ideas most people attach themselves to when it comes to manifesting their dream partner:

How the Relationship Will Manifest

When you put expectations on a relationship before it has even really started, you put pressure on the other person, which creates a sense of dependency that repels most people, especially the kind you want to attract. You can't hide your feelings. We all have the ability (some without even realizing it) to read each other's energy through non-verbal communication. This is why the other person will know if you are feeling needy. You cannot *not* communicate how you really feel at the energetic level. The point is - if you move too fast or force a situation to happen, it'll never naturally escalate. This desperate feeling will repel any potential suitor.

If you force yourself onto someone who you are madly attracted to right off the bat, and they are not feeling the same way, there's going to be resistance. The better way to do it is to not set any expectations of how the relationship will manifest, and instead, learn to just enjoy the moment with them without needing any of your expectations to be fulfilled.

This explains why it is a lot easier to attract someone who you're not all that attracted to because you never gave them that 'needy' vibrational feeling. Usually, neediness repels people and drives them away. If they are not repelled, it's probably going to be an unhealthy, codependent relationship.

Forcing a connection to happen between two people is like trying to plug a USB cord into an electrical outlet. It'll never fit.

If you keep forcing it, not only will you repel the other person that much sooner, but you may also develop a feeling of rejection and sense of unworthiness if you're unaware of your vibrational output. There are times where people just need time to get a feel of who you really are. Not everyone is excited about diving headfirst into a relationship. Take it one step and one connection at a time. After all, you don't *need* this relationship. To bring the point home, take the journey lightly and have fun, it's not serious. The one for you will come in due time, and it'll feel more naturally progressive than anything you've ever felt before.

Another thing to note is that your manifestations come from the unknown. They are something new, different, exciting, and sometimes slightly uncomfortable. If they were coming from the known, you wouldn't feel that exhilarated feeling. Only the universe is responsible for how it's going to manifest. Your only responsibility is taking control of your inner state and allowing the manifestations to come to you.

When the Relationship Will Manifest

The second thing to detach from is when the relationship will manifest. Many men and women get pressured by their relatives to find a mate, settle down, and start a new life. This kind of pressure can actually make the manifestation backfire, or worse, get you into a relationship that you later regret.

Your dream relationship will manifest in divine timing. The universe knows who it is already and could be waiting for you to get your vibrational act together so that you two can meet. But you've got to stop worrying about when it's going to happen because worry is a low vibrational frequency. Worry is a useless emotion when you understand how the universe works.

Only the universe knows when the best time to show you your desire is. You can't control physical reality. You can only control how you respond to it. You will manifest what you desire when you are ready and a vibrational match to it.

Have patience. Manifestations have a delay effect because matter is extremely dense, unlike our thoughts or emotions, which we can feel instantly. When you are feeling good or in alignment, recognize that this is the only proof you need to know that your dream partner is on their way. Literally nothing else matters. Once you've lifted this weight off your shoulder, no external circumstance will ever serve as a metric for possibility or timing. These things are out of your control, which means your manifestation can happen even when you least expect it to. This also means the manifestation of your dream relationship can come sooner than you think, especially if you've been consistently working on becoming a vibrational match to it.

Attracting One Specific Person

Many of us get caught up in the idea that there is only one person for us out there in the world, but that's simply not the case. This romanticized concept of love is the result of the Hollywood movies that we've been portrayed throughout our childhood and adult lives.

This idea that there is only one person out there for us goes against the idea of an abundant mindset. If you're so fixated with attracting one person, you're attached to this one outcome. And if it doesn't work out, then you'll likely feel devastated and unworthy. Focusing on just one person will create unnecessary resistance, especially if you're participating in the act of chasing after them. Even if it does work out, do you really want to be in a relationship where you are solely dependent on the love of one person? Why put yourself in the victim role? You are a powerful creator, and nothing should constrain you from being your best at all times.

If you want to attract just one person, you're also rejecting the infinite number of outcomes the universe has in store for you. Thus, you're creating resistance with your true desire (the feeling of mutual love between you and a dream partner). Attracting one specific person is indeed possible, but it would require so much vibrational sacrifice that it would never be worth it. Most of the time, you would have to tune your frequency to match exactly the person you want to attract by disregarding most of your truth and potential, instead of just being you.

Like the old saying goes, there are plenty of fish in the sea. What if the universe wants to give you a relationship that's even deeper, more passionate, and more fulfilling than this specific one you're so desperately after? Would you reject it? Obviously not. Stay open to infinite possibilities and opportunities.

"Love is detachment, detachment is love."
– Bentinho Massaro

TECHNIQUE #10: SOFTENING THOUGHTS

The main premise for this technique is to simply soften the intensity in which we label, judge, and define other people. This is a particularly powerful technique for those that vet people very heavily when they're dating, express jealousy towards other couples, or judge themselves and others for being who they are.

The idea is simple, when you catch yourself creating a story to define another person, soften this thought process. In other words, think thoughts that go against the original thought that you were thinking.

Here is an example of how you could counter your original thought when judging a couple.

Original Thought: "Look at how perfect they are together. Nobody should be able to be that happy and in love. That's a fairy tale dream that I'll never have."

Softening Thought: "They weren't born together, so they must have been in the same spot I'm in at one point. Which means there is a possibility for me to be just as happy and in love as they are."

Notice how the softening thought detaches you from your original perspective of the situation.

Here is another example.

Original Thought: "Ugh, he likes to watch hockey. That's a deal breaker for me. There's no chance I'm introducing him to my friends and family."

Softening Thought: "Sure, he likes to watch hockey, but he has other qualities that I really enjoy and admire. I appreciate those qualities and I'd like to experience them more."

The best way to avoid an extreme perspective on either side of the thinking spectrum is by keeping your perspective neutral and following the subtle cues of your intuition. In other words, **do not create mental narratives about who someone is and will become.** Instead, let yourself be guided to a decision on a vibrational, emotional, and energetic level. Give your intuition the space it needs to make the best decision for you.

TECHNIQUE #11: LETTING GO OF MISALIGNMENT

Often times, many people stay in relationships with others simply due to the idea that "something is better than nothing." This can be an extremely detrimental perspective because it not only stops you from going after something better, but it can potentially get you to something worse.

The main purpose of this technique is to help you give yourself permission to let go of relationships that are not working out. If you feel like you've been putting up with certain people, sacrificing things you love, and halting your own personal growth for the sake of others, this is the time to reflect.

Think back to how this person or these people make you feel when you're around them. Do they support you unconditionally in reaching the potential you're striving for? Do you feel uplifted after every interaction with them? Do you look forward to interacting with them? Are they in alignment with what you want in this type of relationship?

If you answered 'no' to any of the questions I've asked, consider limiting the amount of energy you invest in the relationship. It can sometimes feel like you're moving away from what you want when you let go of something you've invested so much time into but, the reality of it is, you're actually taking a step forward towards what you truly want. This is because you'll be giving yourself room and space to be living in the frequency of your desire. When you're investing and focusing your energy on relationships that don't make you feel good, guess what? You'll continue to attract relationships that don't make you feel good.

Take this time to write down and review all of the relationships in your life.

"*There are people that love you and there are people that hate you, yet none of that has anything to do with you.*"

– Abraham Hicks

CHAPTER 7

Magnetic Receptivity: How to Receive and Be Open to the Best Relationships

What is the receiving mode *exactly*? What blocks it, and how can you 'unblock' it? Why is having fun so important when it comes to manifesting the love of your life? And how can you ride the wave of positive momentum in order to attract your soul mate?

Let's find out...

THE RECEIVING MODE

The receiving mode is our natural state of being. When we were born, we knew our worthiness. We sensed that receiving was a normal and natural process. When we asked for something, often times, it was given. When we needed anything, often times, we received it. But then, as we got older, society, our parents, and the educational system started to teach us that we needed to *prove* our worthiness instead of enjoying and embracing the receiving mode.

Life is obviously not handed to us on a silver platter. We do need to work and take inspired action to get what we desire. **The problem occurs when we lose sight of the concept that life is supposed to be good to us and that we are supposed to have fun.** Most of us start to buy into the vibration of scarcity, fear, worry, and concern - which is the default vibrational frequency of society in general. We are too "realistic", and allow our fears to stifle our hopes and dreams. This in turn alters our own vibrational frequency.

When we buy into these lower vibrations, when we accept it as the 'normal' way to be, it's hard to get back to our original understanding that we were born worthy and that receiving is normal. It's hard to believe that all we have to do is to ask, and it is given. Most of us have all kinds of evidence to prove that the opposite is true. When we have been programmed to believe that life is a struggle and difficult, it's not easy to suddenly believe the opposite.

Life is all about your perspective, and when your perspective is limiting and disempowering, it's only natural for you to experience this. That is the challenge for all of us, but in order to be, do, and have whatever we want, including attracting the relationships we want, we must embrace what we knew at an early age.

The reason you may not be manifesting your true desires is because something is blocking your manifestations. Since we already know that creation first starts with a thought, it only makes sense that our thinking, negative programming, and unconscious patterns are the reasons for the resistance and blockage.

FOUR MAIN LOVE MANIFESTATION BLOCKS

There are four main reasons why your desired manifestations are being blocked:

Thinking Negative Thoughts

When you think a negative thought and ponder on it, you attract more thoughts that match that vibration. Identifying with any thought, whether it be positive or negative, creates attachment, and when we're attached, we create resistance. This resistance comes because we've stopped going with the natural flow of experience. The more you limit yourself with definitions, labels, and meanings, the more you resist your infinite nature. Most of us cannot help but to think negative thoughts because we've associated our reality with external events and circumstances, either current or those from the past. When you realize that you always have the option to choose a better thought, which gives you a better feeling, at any time, you'll begin changing your reality from the inside out. This is your power.

Feeling Negative Emotions

In general, a thought originates first, and then manifests into an emotion. Your emotions let you know whether your inner being is in alignment with the thought you were just thinking. When you attach yourself to a thought your inner being doesn't agree with, you instantly feel the discord, the misalignment, and that's why you feel the negative emotion.

Your feelings are the gateway to your connection with your inner being, and also the gateway to all of your manifestations, including the relationship you desire.

Reacting vs. Responding

The difference between reacting and responding is that reacting is your old, programmed, knee-jerk impulse to external events that take place in the moment. Reacting is about giving up control over your thoughts and vibration to the pre-conceived notions your ego or subconscious mind wants you to believe.

Responding, on the other hand, is having the awareness to head-off the thought with your inner being's perspective. It's about knowing that all is well and that there is insight to be found even when you experience what you don't want.

Reacting can lower your vibration and allow you to be vulnerable to external, outside conditions, whereas responding keeps your inner state as the priority, resulting in higher vibrational living.

Refusing to Accept a Manifestation

Some people refuse to accept a manifestation. An example of this, is when you meet a wonderful potential partner, but keep imagining every single reason as to why it can't work out with them.

Usually, we refuse to accept a good, healthy manifestation because our subconscious mind is still operating from the old paradigm. Either it wants us to believe that we are unworthy, relationships are problematic, or any other reason why we believe, from past experience, that we shouldn't take the step forward of accepting our manifestation. The key is to learn to let go of the old patterns of thinking and to embrace your physical reality and what your inner being is trying to tell you.

The bottom line is, you need to let go of your attachment to this 'perfect' someone - because they don't exist. Imperfection is where the magic is. When you want to manifest, you should desire the feeling the manifestation will give you, rather than the manifestation itself. Follow the guide of your intuition and not of your thoughts. Follow how someone makes you feel, not what you think of them. When you do this, you open yourself up to a whole new realm of possibility.

HOW TO UNBLOCK THE RECEIVING MODE

You can unblock the receiving mode by shifting your attention and focus onto things (physical or non-physical) that raise your vibration. This takes a little getting used to.

Practically speaking, what this means is when something 'bad' happens to you, such as when someone rejects you, you choose to think a more positive thought. Choosing to neutralize the negative thought by minimizing the importance of the event is also another powerful approach. Give the event a different meaning than you normally would. You don't have to allow your subconscious mind to run the automatic program of defining people and experiences for you.

The point is, *you* have the control to choose whatever thought you want, whenever you want. You could choose to think happy thoughts at any time you want. If nothing exciting is happening in physical reality, bring your focus to the non-physical (your imagination), and vice-versa.

There is one important point to realize. Do not expect to make a huge leap from negative, pessimistic, and disempowering thinking, to suddenly being the eternal optimist who is always happy. Rather, take it one easy step at a time, one perspective at a time, until you finally start recognizing the bigger picture.

An example of this is if you're feeling fearful of something, you cannot expect yourself to think your way into a more courageous feeling. Instead, learn to accept the fear by reframing the feeling or event. Ask yourself questions to rationalize the fear. Ask yourself where those thoughts are *actually* coming from and whether they are truly relevant when it comes to manifesting your desire. Notice if you're thinking too much in the past or too much in the future. Bring your focus back to the present moment. This is where the choice of choosing a better feeling thought is made.

Do not get upset if you're unable to instantly rise the ranks of the emotional scale – it's near impossible. It's too far of a vibrational gap between fear and joy. You have to work your way up the emotional scale by using the power of focus.

THE POWER OF FOCUS

If you're not receiving, then your focus is on the fact that you're not receiving. Instead, focus on the receiving part. Focus on experiencing what it is the universe has to offer you and know that it is always to your benefit, whether it's the manifestation itself, or a sign that you need to shift your focus. Challenges should always be welcomed because they give us clues to where we need to improve vibrationally. The discord and disharmony we feel when not in alignment with our true selves are clues that help you improve your perspective around certain areas of your life.

It takes some discipline to purposely focus on thoughts and things that feel good, but it is essential to invoking the power of manifestation. Let's take Bianca's story as an example.

Bianca was single for 13 years. She had always been feeling this need for a relationship and the more she needed it, the longer she went without one. Eventually, this neediness translated into a feeling of unworthiness. The longer you go without a relationship, the more this feeling can pervade. And so, this cycle continued until she learned to shift her focus.

Instead of attaching herself to disempowering ideas related to being single, she began developing a positive free flowing perspective shift that felt perfectly aligned with her inner being. She expected the manifestation of the type of man she wanted to attract, but also let go of the resistance she was building towards it, through awareness of her thoughts and emotions. There were times she felt lonely or doubtful, but this didn't stop her from following her excitement and riding the wave of positive momentum. This search for love ends when she finally decides to be the attraction point of it, and eventually crosses paths with a man she believes to be 'the one.'

A lot of magic can happen when you decide to let go of the resistance that comes with attachment. One of the best ways of doing this is by having fun!

HAVE FUN WITH THE LOVE FINDING PROCESS

Life is supposed to be good to you, and it's also supposed to be fun. You do not need to make the process of attracting your love relationship so serious. If it's serious to you, then you possibly feel threatened by the manifestation not happening. This leads you to vibrating at the frequency of lack, worry, and fear – all wrong frequencies for manifesting the love of your life.

If you're having fun, then you know it's going to happen eventually. Creation happens immediately after you have a desire. Now it's time to become a vibrational match to it in order to make it manifest physically. After you set your vibrational frequency, having received benefit from the contrast of past bad relationships and experiences, you are all set to manifest the relationship you truly want. But remember, you have to become a vibrational match to your mate and that is done by 'being as if' that person is already here. In order to do that, all you have to do is let go of the worry, embody the excitement, and have fun NOW – not later.

When a potential partner sees how happy, fun, and wonderful you are, they will be attracted to you in all aspects – physically, emotionally, mentally and even spiritually. The vibration of neediness or lack, that would normally create resistance, seizes to exist.

Have fun with the process! Be open to testing and trying out new things. Step into the unknown - which means you're in a state of creation and spontaneity. This is the state you want to be in if you're looking for love because love is all about fun, spontaneity, exhilaration, excitement, randomness, and adventure.

Appreciate the things you have when you're single and appreciate the idea and feelings you get with the possibility of you finding love. Remember, the journey on the way to your dream relationship is just as exciting too.

If you're thinking there are other people in your life who stifle your fun vibration, it may be best to stay away from them during this high vibrational fun time in your life. That's right – fun might include avoiding certain people and situations.

Fun is loose, free, and open – the exact vibration that attracts all of your love desires. When you let go and allow yourself to feel that kind of fun, you'll manifest your desired relationship in no time.

RIDING THE WAVE OF POSITIVE MOMENTUM

Momentum, when it really picks up, is one of the most powerful approaches to manifestation. It can turn a year's worth of work, down to a week. And when we're able to master the principles of vibrational momentum, we're able to change our reality at an exhilarating pace.

The best way to start momentum is by following your excitement. When you follow what feels good, you give yourself permission to radiate at the frequency of your desires. This means you're aligned with the perspective of your inner being. In other words, when you do what feels good (not familiar), you become a magnet to more of it. Do things that excite you, because this vibration is the one that matches that of your dream relationship.

Momentum can also be described as the 'snowball effect,' where a small snowball rolling down a snowy hill gathers momentum along the way by becoming larger and larger as it picks up more snow. When the ball is rolling, it will keep on rolling unless it is met with very strong resistance. The longer the momentum goes on, the more powerful it is.

Negative thoughts can, however, also build momentum. Just as you have the power to start positive momentum by stepping into the unknown and having more fun; you also have the power to start negative momentum. **The sooner you stop associating yourself with the negative thoughts that cross your mind, before they become negative emotions – the more chances you have of building your positive momentum.**

You have the power to control your vibrational momentum, whether it's positive or negative. If it's negative, stop it quickly and it won't gain any momentum.

When jumpstarting positive vibrational momentum, without being uninterrupted by contrary or negative thinking, the energy behind your thoughts and emotions start to gain traction. According to inspirational speaker and author Abraham

Hicks, whenever you think a thought for over 17 seconds; it passes a threshold, gains 10 times its strength, and thereby starts attracting more experiences, people, circumstances, and events that match that vibration. And when you keep going on with the positive thought for another 17 seconds without pondering on negative ones, again, it gets 10 times stronger in its attraction power. When you do this for 68 seconds, your attraction power is many, many more times powerful than when you started.

When it comes to applying the power of momentum, many problems often arise. We allow our thoughts to entertain doubt and worry without ever allowing them to gain traction. It's actually very common for most of us to think a resistant thought even while in the middle of a short, brief, positive thought. The challenge is in believing that what you want is coming to you, even if you don't see any physical signs of it happening yet.

Do not allow contrast and negative external manifestations to disrupt your positive momentum. And don't get discouraged if you know that you've been vibing high, but you still see negative things happening in your life. What you are manifesting today may be the result of your vibration a few days ago. Physical reality is delayed compared to the non-physical one. When you recognize this, everything you see, hear, touch, smell, and taste, starts looking more like old news.

Remember - how you feel right here and now, is actually creating your future.

The point is to stick to high vibrational thoughts and feelings and ride this wave to achieve quantum leaps in your love life and beyond.

TECHNIQUE #12: GOOD MORNING MOMENTUM

For this technique, we're going to be bringing attention to the vibrational momentum that you carry throughout the day. There is a saying that goes like this:

"Take thy thoughts to bed with thee, for the morning is wiser than the evening"

In the morning, our vibration, thoughts, and emotions are fully reset. In other words, there are no filters or momentum to alter and stagnate our focus. Every morning is the perfect opportunity to align your focus with your desires. It's the time of day where you get to choose how you will feel for the rest of the day. Will you continue to sob about the problems of yesterday or focus on the creation of today? Do you want to continue having the negative momentum or do you want to build new positive momentum?

Here are three tips to help you master your morning:

1. Avoid things that can potentially start you off with negative momentum. These things can include the news, emails, social media, and work-related things.
2. Have a reminder to check in on where your focus is. Have a daily morning practice like meditation, journaling, reading, or visualization, in order to start off in the right momentum. If it involves exercising, reading a book, or looking at a vision board, set everything up the night before.
3. Dedicate your morning to high vibrational thoughts and perspectives related to love. The morning is the perfect time

to build a new self-image and embody a new version of you... an identity that is loved, secure, whole, magnetic, excited, optimistic, attractive, confident, and appreciative.

4. Practice doing things you would do as if your partner was already here. For example: Make a little bit of extra coffee, visualize yourself waking up next to someone, or even say "good morning" out loud when getting out of bed or saying "have a good day" before going out to work. This might sound a little bizarre, but it works for many people.

When you fully embody this new version of you, you immediately start emitting a new frequency, thus attracting a new reality.

TECHNIQUE #13: MIRRORING LOVE

We've talked in length about visualization and how you should be focusing more on the traits and personality of the person you want to attract rather than their physical appearance. For this technique, we're going to take this a step forward.

In persuasion psychology, there is a technique called mirroring. This involves mimicking the behavior of the other person in order to gain influence and get them to like you. If you've ever noticed two good friends, you'll see that they behave, talk, and act in a very similar fashion. They've become accustomed to mirroring each other's behaviors. This is a natural instinct that humans have to help them bond and connect with others in a community. Mirroring is a technique for building rapport, and people are attracted to people they have rapport with.

By using the Mirroring Love technique, we're not going to be mirroring anything in your physical reality. Instead, we're going to be mirroring your desired partner in your imagination. For example, if you wish to attract someone that is outgoing, fun, and affectionate, take the time to imagine what this person would be like. Think about how they behave and act. After you've imagined what they would be like, simply mirror this in your mind.

When you shift your mental focus using this technique, you're building the belief that this person is out there. When you rehearse this enough, you will automatically translate the rapport you were building mentally to your physical reality. Not only will you attract the person you want, but you'll know exactly how to behave when the universe brings you this opportunity. Since you've already been dating this person mentally, the manifestation of your desired relationship is inevitable.

Take this time now to write down and imagine how your desired partner behaves and acts. Carry on with your life while keeping this in mind and continue rehearsing your interactions with them in your imagination.

"To fear love is to fear life, and those who fear life are already three parts dead."

– Bertrand Russel

CHAPTER 8

Dating Traps: How to Let Go of Fear and Avoid Bad Relationships

In this chapter, we're going to cover how to get over any fear around dating and accidently attracting bad relationships. Many of us unconsciously reject love when it presents itself because subconsciously, we fear stepping into this new reality. On the other end, we unconsciously accept bad relationships because they're familiar to us.

FEAR OF THE UNKNOWN

If you feel fearful when it comes to receiving and entering a new relationship, rest assured that it's completely normal. Why? Because a new relationship is NEW. It's the unknown. It's uncomfortable because you haven't physically experienced it yet. If this is the case and if you don't feel ready, then you probably aren't. And this is okay - you'll soon find out why.

The way to move past this is to understand the following:

Your Manifestations Come from the Unknown

Your manifestation will never come from the known. This is because if it came from the known, it would come from the old identity. If the old identity only attracted bad relationships, then that's exactly what it'll keep attracting. If the old identity never attracted a relationship, then it'll never attract a relationship. The known is old and the unknown is new.

You're Never Going to Feel Ready

Because everything is coming from the unknown, it'll always be a new experience that you've never experienced before in physical reality. This means that if you decide to take the leap into a new relationship, it'll feel different, new, exciting, and adventurous. Grab the feelings of fear or 'unreadiness' and reframe it into *excitement*. Imagine it being like you're walking through a door into a whole new reality of your life where your desired relationship exists. Don't worry about tripping over yourself or committing errors, this is part of the frequency calibrating process. Be excited about the experience and confirm to yourself that you've manifested what you want.

Don't be too Specific About What You're Getting Into

If it feels new, different, and adventurous, leave it at that. Leave it at the emotional level. If this new relationship feels easy, spontaneous and comforting, leave it as an easy, spontaneous, and comforting relationship. Stop thinking about specifics of the situation such as, "What will my friends think?", "What will my parents think?", "Is this person really my (ego's) type?", or "What if they break my heart?"

Leave it at a general level and enjoy it for what it is *now*. An example of a general statement might be, "It's exciting to start dating again," or, "That was a fun date and maybe I'd like to go out again." When you get too specific too fast, you risk lowering your vibration because you're diving too deeply into rationality and realism. There's a time and place for this, but when it takes over your entire experience, you're not letting the magic unfold in the way it should. Feel the difference between the vibration of "It would be nice to go out on a date again and have a good time," versus "That was a nice date, but I wonder if they are ready for commitment, if my mother and family would like them, and if they make enough money." When you start to go down the path of being too specific, you risk lowering your vibration. And when it comes to attracting your dream relationship, we need to approach it with unconditional love, to then be presented with the conditions.

Use your intuition to feel your way into the relationship, instead of your analytical and egoic mind that subconsciously doesn't want you to risk letting go of the familiar.

INTUITION VS FEAR

When do you know a relationship is worth pursuing? How do you know if it's the right one?

If you're not in a vibrational match with your desired relationship, no matter how many times you bypass the fear mechanism, the relationship you're jumping into will not be the one you desire. **Action does not replace vibrational alignment.** It can certainly help you reach vibrational alignment, but it does not replace it entirely. If your vibrational frequency is out of alignment, you will attract someone that matches that energetic signature, regardless if you take physical action towards something better.

On the other hand, if you keep rejecting people and saying 'no' to opportunities, you may simply be fearful of the situation, but mistaking it for your intuition.

How do you separate the two? How do you know the difference?

Add the concept of time...

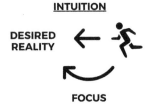

If your initial decision is 'yes' to the relationship, become aware of the underlying place this answer is coming from. Is it coming from a place of "I've missed many opportunities in the past so I have to say yes to this one" or is it coming from "This feels exciting. It may not feel totally comfortable, but it feels passionate, expansive, and fun at this very moment, which is exactly what I'm looking for."

The first phrase has the concept of time, meaning it is coming from an egoic way of thinking rather than from the perspective of your inner being. The second phrase doesn't take time into the equation because the decision is made from the present moment and from intuitive awareness.

If your initial decision is 'no,' become aware of the underlying place this answer is coming from. Is it coming from a place of "I've met people like him/her before and I'm sure we'll never work out together" or is it coming from a place of "I'm still trying to feel this person out but at this moment in time, it just does not feel right and I feel limited/non-expansive/unexcited when I'm around them."

Compare these two, and notice if there is the concept of time. In other words, make a decision from the intuitive hunches you feel in the present moment, *not* from the past or future.

The difference between intuition and fear is that intuition does not require logical thought. Fear, on the other hand, is an illusion that is built out of our egoic and biased logic.

You can't walk in fear and expect magical things to happen. Those who succeed, take steps forward with full faith that they are going to manifest what they want, no matter how their physical reality looks. Push forward in faith, and not fear.

STOP SAVING SOMEONE ELSE

It is very common for some of us to get into relationships where it's one sided – where you are doing all you can in order to keep things going smoothly, but your partner is not. At the heart of the problem are limiting beliefs that can keep a person stuck in a relationship, doing all they can to make it right, while the other person puts little to no intention into it.

These limited beliefs are usually feelings like, "I'm not good enough," or "I can fix him/her," or feelings of insecurity before and during the relationship. It could also be an unhealthy codependent relationship that puts you in a vicious cycle of breaking up and making up.

Hear this clearly now. **Do not enter a relationship if you're going to be the one carrying all the weight.** And when I say weight, I mean emotional, mental, and even financial. A relationship with an unequal balance of energy investment is not a relationship. It is draining for both people, and not only for the one pulling most of the weight. It's okay to be there when someone is having a hard time, but this can't be a normal pattern.

For example, if your partner just lost their job, it's okay to take up the financial responsibility for a while until they get back up on their feet. This is normal, and if anything, it shows that commitment is there. During this time, they can try and compensate in other areas, like taking care of the house chores or cooking the meals.

But if your partner doesn't get off the couch to get another job, or if they don't do anything to make up for the lost wages, then there could be a serious problem in the relationship. Your partner may become sad and depressed from the job loss, which is normal, but they may also be using that as an excuse to not pull their own weight in the relationship. When there is an energy imbalance, you really have to acknowledge it, attempt to do something about it, and take action if it can't be resolved.

Anyone can fall into the trap of doing too much for the other person because of feelings of obligation, duty, or even to save face in order to not have to deal with the supposed embarrassment that can come with a breakup. This eagerness to save someone else may have come from past moments in early childhood, when one was forced to take up the parent or caregiver role. When this happens, people can unconsciously carry this into their relationships.

Even when you're dating you can notice imbalances in energy investments. For example, if you find yourself paying for all the meals, picking out all the places and activities, and initiating all the conversations, there's clearly an imbalance. Discuss this with the other person if you feel comfortable about it, or simply throw the ball into their court by not initiating. If you notice they're not interested in investing, it's probably not a good match.

Approach every relationship from the powerful perspective that even if you can love unconditionally, you deserve to be happy in it, and that if the relationship is not growing spiritually, mentally, or emotionally, then it may be dying.

However, it is also not a good idea to keep track of every little thing they do or not do in order to keep a scorecard of how they are doing. Just keep things balanced the best way you can without keeping score. Keeping score creates unnecessary tension, and can leave someone uncomfortable if they're not fully capable of providing what you want at that moment. Give each other options, be creative, and build the relationship *together.*

BE CLEAR ON
WHAT YOU WANT

One of the biggest reasons people do not attract the right relationship for them is because they simply do not know what kind of relationship they want. In previous chapters, we've talked about how to use bad past experiences as a guide for the creation of good future ones. We established the point that contrast, or the 'bad' things that happened in your past relationships, helped you to be clear on what you do not want so that you could be clear as to what you do want.

If you let all of these 'bad' signs pass you by without taking them into account, you'll only be running into the same problem again and again. You can't attract a better relationship without mentally and emotionally changing how you approach them. Create boundaries, set standards, discover new feelings etc. until you've constructed a mental image and emotional feeling of what your dream relationship would look and feel like for you.

Recognize that without a clear intention of what you want to attract, the Universe will only continue granting to you what you've always been and currently are attracting.

If you do decide to move on from your relationship and find one more suited to what you want, the following discussion is important to understand.

HOW TO HAVE
A POSITIVE BREAKUP

How can you have a positive break-up? Is it even possible? Do you believe it's a given that every relationship break-up has to end up in a huge fight where you vow to hate each other for the rest of your lives?

In order to leave a relationship that no longer feels good to you, it may seem like the best way to do it is to burn it to the ground so neither of you would ever want to try again. But there is one major problem with doing it that way…

If you have bitter, ill feelings about your old relationship, you're going to attract the same kind of relationship once again via the Law of Attraction. **On every subject matter in life, you are a current vibrational match to wherever you last left your vibration relative to the topic.** If you last left it in a low vibrational point, then you're going to attract the same kind of relationship once again, unless you become aware of this. If you want to attract a positive relationship, you have to re-think and find a way - ANY way - to appreciate the last relationship and mean it. Remember, the universe doesn't hear the words coming out of your mouth – it responds to how you *feel*.

Most people, when they realize that this is how it works, think that if they leave the old relationship with a positive perspective, they will be tempted to go back to it, which defeats the whole purpose in leaving to begin with. But it doesn't have to be that way. That is simply a belief that most of us have on how to have a breakup. You can leave a past relationship from a place

of appreciation, gratitude, and thankfulness when you decide to
see it from a positive perspective.

THE 3 LAYERS
OF A RELATIONSHIP

Relationships can sometimes feel like the most complex topic
in the world. And when you look at all of the components that
come with one, it's no reason why many people struggle. In
this subchapter, I've decided to breakdown a relationship into
3 simple layers. Each layer will cover a certain perspective, but
ultimately, only one should serve as a guidepost. When you fully
grasp these concepts, you'll find it easier when it comes time to
make the decision on whether it's worth committing to or not.

Chemistry

Chemistry between people can be defined as the amount of
positive polarity tension that exists between them. Tension is
similar to magnetism and the more polarized the energy is, the
stronger the attraction. Chemistry is evident between people
who naturally work, exist, and simply flow together. You cannot
create or destroy natural chemistry, though it is fluid. It can be
built up or broken down but will always remain between people
who have it.

Compatibility

Compatibility is something we filter through our logical minds,
to determine whether a person has the potential of being 'the

one.' We base these thoughts and beliefs on society's assumptions that if we meet someone who has the same traits and beliefs as us, comes from the same area, had the same type of upbringing, and enjoys the same things, for example, that it must be a perfect match. However, if you have not embraced your limitless and unique expression, the factors you are basing your beliefs about compatibility on will not work – and seldom do - for anyone. That is because they do not reflect your truth.

You do not need to be compatible to have a deep connection with someone. In other words, you do not need to have the same interests, same background, logical matches, or similarities to feel the loving connection between one another. Do not choose partners out of logical deduction. Remember, when it comes to attracting your dream relationship, we need to bait from the heart, and not from the mind.

Connection

Connection is more important than compatibility. That's because we use our logical minds to deduce who we consider ourselves to be compatible with, while connection comes from our heart and intuitive senses. Connection is best evident in friends and loved ones who might not have seen each other for a long time, but simply 'pick up where they left off' when they meet up again. Connection is the reason many couples seem to have a surprisingly good relationship, even though they seemingly have low compatibility, from a societal or outsiders' perspective.

Connection is either there or it's not. Within connection, there is chemistry. If you have chemistry with someone, this doesn't necessarily mean there is a connection though. For example, you might have chemistry with co-workers to get a job done right, but this doesn't necessarily mean you have to like them or have a connection with them.

Problems in relationships occur when the deciding factor, for whether to commit to it or not, revolves solely around compatibility and other external factors. This is usually due to having limited beliefs that lead to rash decisions and assumptions. External expectations and judgment normally have the biggest influence. This is why having a strong sense of self BEFORE you get into a relationship is key to having a good one. **You do not need to change who you are. All you need to do is show more of it and less of what you are not.**

Connection will always include chemistry, but not necessarily compatibility – and that's okay. Because compatibility is a societal perception…but chemistry and connection are felt within. **It is connection that you are after**.

It doesn't need to make logical sense. It needs to make emotional sense. And when you give yourself the power to intuitively make relationship decisions, you let go of all assumptions, and allow the universe to work its magic on you.

TECHNIQUE #14: YOU'LL KNOW WHEN YOU KNOW

How many times have you walked into a room and scanned every single person inside, asking yourself whether they are the one you've been looking for? How many times have you vetted people superficially before even giving them a chance? How many times have you talked yourself into wanting a relationship with someone you don't really want a relationship with? For this technique, we're going to bring awareness to that inspired impulse that lets you know when a certain person you've been seeing is the one you've been wanting to attract. Recognize that not everyone will fit exactly with what you want. Your only job is to be in alignment with yourself and your desires regardless of what's going on outside of you. When you're in alignment, you're a vibrational match to who you want to attract, and thus the decisions you make will follow these criteria.

How different do you think love feels when it comes from the mind compared to when it comes from the heart? Very different! In fact, there will be very little resistance on your part and on the other person's part when your love comes from the heart. The connection between you two will be effortless. That is to say, the attraction between you two will not come from a place of neediness, negative expectation, or doubt. It will come from an intuitive place where both of you are in alignment with who you both are. You'll be inspired to spend more time with this person, not motivated to do it. Your conversations will flow, the physical attraction will be effortless, and spending time with each other will feel like magic and creation.

The focus will always be on the fun, expansion, spontaneity, appreciation, and love for each other. This does not mean there will not be hard times ahead. With expansion, comes challenges, but with these challenges, come growth and even more love. You won't ever need to try and 'make it work' or work through hard times. All of the moments, including the bad ones, will feel effortlessly progressive. This is when you know you've found your match.

Love is instant and immediate. It does not take time. When it takes time it's because you've learned to tolerate it and are afraid of throwing away weeks or months of time and energy investment.

Your inner being knows when there is potential. It defies logic. Follow your heart.

"Love is not something that is a sort of rare commodity, everyone has it."

– Alan Watts

CHAPTER 9

Love Manifestation Essentials

There are three essential things you need to know and implement into your life in order to manifest the love you want. When you understand and apply these principles, attracting the loving relationship you desire will feel effortless and you'll have a lot more fun doing it too.

PATIENCE AND TRUST

Generally speaking, a patient person is more in alignment with the relationship they want than an impatient one. This is because they do not offer up a resistant, impatient vibration that leads to forced actions and uninspired decisions. When you are impatient, you introduce doubt and worry into your vibration, which blocks the relationship you truly want from manifesting.

A patient person does not worry about how, when, why, or if a relationship will happen; they just know it will. The frequency of knowing is just one step above the frequency of believing, because when you know, it's because the manifestation is inevitable. Whether it happens tomorrow, next week, or next year, they're not worried about that. They understand their focus should purely be on themselves and how they are feeling in the present moment in relation to this desired relationship.

An impatient person, on the other hand, radiates vibrations of neediness, dependency, and lack. They're impatient because they doubt the manifestation of their desire. When there is doubt, it's because they may feel unworthy to manifest it. It's a clear signal they haven't done the work internally. This is why it hasn't shown up externally. An impatient person will ignore their intuition, make bad choices, and repel the type of love they're truly after. They are always looking for a predictable path, the opposite of what true manifestation is. All of this resistance will not lead to anything fulfilling.

There is a third way to be, however, and that is to not even need patience. Someone who is very conscious about the process of manifestation knows they are able to create the feeling of what is wanted now. This is because they are aware that the creation of what they want requires one to feel the feeling of it FIRST. If you must feel the feeling first, and the feeling is the whole reason why you want anything anyway, then the feeling is a manifestation in and of itself – something you can create RIGHT NOW. And if you can create that feeling right now, then why would you need patience?

Of course, we all love the actual, physical manifestation of what it is we want. The point is that you really only need patience when you're not having a good day, or are out of alignment with who you really are. Then, yes, patience is needed. But when you are living at a high vibrational frequency and feeling great, you don't need patience because there is nothing to wait for, vibrationally speaking.

When you worry about what you want (the physical aspect) not coming quickly enough, you offer up resistance to the universe. Resistant thoughts and feelings delay any physical manifestation, and that's the 'Catch-22' situation many of us find ourselves in. When you are desperate for something, you are resistant to it, and when you are resistant to it, you delay its manifestation.

Patience brings the knowingness that the universe will only deliver when you're vibrationally ready, and when the timing is right. Until then, appreciate the moments that bring clarity to what you want and what you don't want in a relationship. Trust that when the time is right, the universe will deliver. Know that the universe won't deliver unless you are a vibrational match. The focus should therefore always be on becoming a more confident, open, and limitless version of yourself.

Understand that the joy you're looking for actually comes from the *journey* of manifesting your dream relationship. The journey is *now*. Pure desire is the fuel that keeps you going; letting go of any emotional baggage or disempowering beliefs will remove any resistance; and when you do these two things, the manifestation will come effortlessly. **Want without needing, expect without attaching, and know without doubting.**

When we talk about having patience, this does not mean you need to wait for things to change. Expect change to happen, without being attached to how it will occur, by taking the initiative of working on your vibration. Have what I like to call *eager patience*. This is a feeling of anticipation without doubt and worry about the who, what, when, and where. It's the feeling of good, positive expectation – a high vibrational frequency. In this state, inspired action flourishes.

Develop a vibrational commitment to living at the frequency of your desire. In other words, look forward to the manifestation because you already know it's going to happen. You're eager to step into this new reality and start living it, but with a certain understanding that the universe will time it just perfectly for you. You know you are vibrationally preparing for the manifestation. When your dream partner finally shows up, you may not even realize it because you were living it the whole time. This physical manifestation felt natural and in alignment with who you were already being.

Do not disguise the action of waiting with the word 'patience'. When you do this, you're devising an excuse for why your manifestation hasn't happened yet. In other words, through the feeling of 'waiting,' you're looking for reasons outside of you for why it hasn't happened yet. In other words, you're covering up the fact that you're not in a vibrational match with what you desire. This is a loophole that many people fall into and it's very important to be aware of this.

MASTERING LONELINESS AND SOLITUDE

Loneliness is the idea of being in solitude from a scarcity mindset point of view. Just the word 'lonely' conjures up images of a 'sad and gloomy' person, with no friends or family, who has reached a very low point in life. But on the opposite side of this coin could be someone who has purposely chosen to 'be alone' in order to gain clarity, to connect with themselves, and to connect to source energy. For example, meditation is best done alone, yet there is no association of sadness or loneliness with it.

There is a misconception about what loneliness is because society has labeled it as something that is bad or downgrading. It's viewed as a negative to spend time alone. What most people think of loneliness is something like, "If I'm lonely, it's because nobody likes me," or, "If I'm lonely, it's because there is something wrong with me." All of us have been programmed to believe that in most contexts, being alone equates to loneliness. But that's a limited belief you can change.

Perception is everything, and the only perception that matters is yours. I'm not saying you should strive for being alone; what I'm saying is that being alone doesn't mean you need to be out of alignment.

Loneliness is a feeling that comes based on the definition we give to it. What if we thought of loneliness as something positive? What if we started to interpret loneliness rather as it being the perfect time for us to align with our inner being without external distractions? In other words, it's the perfect time to look within and fill all the voids we have with what we already have within us. Nothing on the outside can fill the void of feeling lonely. You can feel full right here and right now, even if there is nobody around you.

EVERYONE IS IN THE SAME LEAGUE

Have you ever met someone who you were very attracted to, and then found yourself thinking of them as the 'one and only one,' or the 'perfect love' you were waiting for your entire life, before you even actually got to know them? That's the act of putting someone on a pedestal. When you put someone on a pedestal, what you tell the universe and what you non-verbally communicate to the other person is you are not worthy of them, or not good enough. When you feel that way, the admired one can feel it too, and then, they, in turn, immediately turn off towards you. It's over before it even started.

It's very difficult sometimes to communicate how you really feel with words alone. The exact emotion that is fueling your energy can only be sensed and not described. This is important to understand because it tells us that your self-image is the most important thing when it comes to building attraction with another person. **How you feel about yourself makes all the difference in the world.**

When you feel like you are on their level; that they are simply the next logical step for you, and you are worthy of someone so wonderful because you too are wonderful; they will pick up on that feeling. They will get the sense you are their equal, and subsequently feel the attraction at the same level.

You should never put anyone on any kind of a pedestal. It's hard to do when you are really physically attracted to someone and when your emotions course powerfully through your veins, but as you build more self-awareness, it becomes easier and easier.

When you see someone else as 'out of your league,' you unintentionally vibrationally place yourself away from them. In other words, you no longer vibrationally resonate with them, hence, this is why they are not attracted to you and you are not magnetic to them.

Looking down on someone is also not an option. When you do this, you close yourself off to beautiful people that can provide you with just as much love as anyone else can. **Be open, be free to engage and interact, and always carry with you the realization that we are one.**

In order to be magnetic to a certain kind of person, you need to be at the same level as them vibrationally – not higher or lower – meaning, you need to feel neither superior nor inferior to them. If you feel superior, you'll live at a state of being that makes them no longer want to be around you because you energetically put them down. If you feel inferior, you'll live at a state of being that makes them want to pursue someone 'better.' People can feel your energy! They can feel how you feel about you.

The take home lesson here is this: **Nobody is out of your league because everybody is in the *same* league.** We are so much more similar than not. No one is better or worse than you, which means that *anyone* is a possibility if you so choose.

The point is that foundationally, we are all the same. The only difference we have between each other is how we show up in the world. Never assume or label anyone with a rank or status. This way, people will relate to you more as they sense your openness, because you're no longer viewing them as an egoic separate identity, but as another extension of you. When you do this, you become receptive to so many more people than you thought possible. **You become magnetic**.

TECHNIQUE #15:
LETTER TO SELF

Mastering the power of positive self-talk is a skill that will allow you to move through your reality without ever being fazed by what's in front of you. For this technique, we're going to be moving this positive self-talk from your head onto a piece of paper.

This letter will not come from your present self, but rather the future self you are inspired to become. In other words, embody the future version of yourself when you are writing this letter. Notable figures like Arnold Schwarzenegger and Bruce Lee have used a similar technique to achieve their goals and ambitions.

The aim of this is to provide you with a record of you reminding yourself of who you truly are and the potential you have to manifest anything you desire. Whenever you're feeling low, heartbroken, or pessimistic, take out this letter and read it. This is a sure and easy way to lift your mood because it removes all of the ego filters that are blocking your true self from speaking to you inside of your head.

Follow the steps outlined below to ensure that your letter is as effective as possible:

1. Get yourself into a high vibrational frequency before writing this letter. It must come from a place of inspiration and not motivation.
2. Write down the date you expect to experience these life changes. Expectation is a desire combined with a belief that it will come true. Put intention into the words you are writing.

3. Write in the present tense. Avoid talking about what you will do, and start talking about what you are doing.

4. Express vivid details of how your life has panned out. Do you have a family? How many kids? Where are living? Visualize the love life you've always wanted.

5. Talk about the elevated emotions you are feeling. How happy, excited, and fulfilled do you feel?

6. Avoid talking about anything that is negative. Bring yourself into abundance instead of out of lack.

Conclusion

There is a powerful non-physical part of you that is connected to the infinite layers and dimensions spread across all of the cosmos. When you realize who you truly are, and how life is meant to be for you, then attracting love not only becomes effortless, but the journey to your dream relationship becomes enjoyable as well.

Realize that you must first become that which you want to manifest. Life is an inside game – you don't have to hammer it all into place. Manifesting is a process which requires work from the inside, out. Remove your focus from extrinsic opinions. You only need to work on recognizing your own true inner being, so that you can begin to shift more into alignment with who you truly are. When you change your outlook on life, your relationships will shift accordingly to match it.

You were born worthy, and you have nothing to prove to your parents, to society, or to your prospective partners. Once you work on loving yourself to the point where you can unconditionally love yourself, only then will you become a vibrational match to the relationship of your dreams. When you get to that vibrational level, and are able to maintain it or shift back into it whenever you fall off, you get that much closer to attracting the love of your life. It's only a matter of divine timing.

Believe it, think it, feel it - and you'll see it. Keep your standards high and never settle. Keep remembering who you really are, a limitless and infinite source of energy. Remind yourself of the value of *you*.

Embody a version of you that is in alignment with exactly the type of partner you desire, and then let the universe do the heavy lifting by naturally and spontaneously bringing you together. You will know when it happens. There will be no doubt. And it will feel like the most natural next step into the best relationship you have ever had before.

Consider yourself fully equipped now. You have done the work; you have acknowledged the changes that need to be made within you to form perfect alignment with yourself, and thus attract an amazing partner. Let go of unnecessary and disempowering attachments, and allow yourself to experience the magic of manifesting love.

Take that step into the new and unknown. Have fun. Your fresh new journey towards your dream relationship has begun.

A Short Message
From The Author

Hey there, did you enjoy the book? Hopefully you did! A lot of work, research, and collaborations took place to make this book what it is today. So if you enjoyed *The Magic of Manifesting Love*, I'd love to hear your thoughts in the review section on Amazon. com. It helps me gain valuable feedback to produce the highest quality content for all of my beautiful readers. Even just a short 1-2 sentence review would mean the WORLD to me.

>> Scan the QR Code below with your smartphone
to leave a short review on Amazon <<

Thank you from the bottom of my heart for purchasing and reading it to end.

Sincerely,